USING AI
IN MARKETING

USING AI
IN MARKETING

An Introduction

By Greg Kihlström

MERCURY LEARNING AND INFORMATION
Boston, Massachusetts

Publisher: David Pallai
MERCURY LEARNING AND INFORMATION
121 High Street, 3rd Floor
Boston, MA 02110
info@merclearning.com
www.merclearning.com
800-232-0223

Greg Kihlström. *Using AI in Marketing: An Introduction.*
ISBN: 978-150152-279-6

The publisher recognizes and respects all marks used by companies, manufacturers, and developers as a means to distinguish their products. All brand names and product names mentioned in this book are trademarks or service marks of their respective companies. Any omission or misuse (of any kind) of service marks or trademarks, etc. is not an attempt to infringe on the property of others.

Library of Congress Control Number: 2024937983
242526321   This book is printed on acid-free paper in the United States of America.

Our titles are available for adoption, license, or bulk purchase by institutions, corporations, etc. For additional information, please contact the Customer Service Dept. at 800-232-0223 (toll free).

To Lindsey,
my partner in agility.

CONTENTS

ACKNOWLEDGMENTS

As with any book, countless people had a hand in the thoughts and ideas contained within this volume. I will endeavor to name at least a few of them, but a full list would comprise its own book, so please excuse this abbreviated list.

First, I want to thank Carlos Manalo, Cofounder and Co-CEO of The Office of Experience for contributing the foreword for this book. Additionally, there are many people I have worked with on AI-based projects, presentations, and initiatives over the past several months, some of which I am able to name, and others I may need to keep confidential. For the sake of brevity, I will simply say a huge "thank you" to everyone I've worked with on consulting engagements and other projects and initiatives.

Thanks to James Walsh and the Mercury Learning team for being so great to work with on the publishing of this book.

Thanks to my parents, including my mother who has always encouraged me to reach for new and bigger opportunities; my father, who although he isn't here to read this book, is always a source of inspiration; as well as my sister Janelle and her family. Thanks also to my wife Lindsey, who always supports me, no matter how many books I write during a year (this year, it will be a few). She is forever an inspiration, and I'm thankful to have such a great partner in all things.

Finally, thanks to everyone reading this book, anyone who has listened to my podcast, read an article or blog post, and supported me in any way over the past several years. I hope that the thoughts and ideas shared by myself, and others have been helpful in your work.

Let's move forward and create great things together!

About the Author

Greg Kihlström is a best-selling author, speaker, and entrepreneur, and serves as an advisor and consultant to top companies on marketing technology, marketing operations, customer experience, and digital transformation initiatives. He has worked with some of the world's top brands, including Adidas, Coca-Cola, FedEx, HP, Marriott, Nationwide, Victoria's Secret, and Toyota.

He is a multiple-time cofounder and C-level leader, leading his digital experience agency to be acquired by the largest independent marketing agency in the Washington DC region in 2017, successfully exited an HR technology platform provider he cofounded in 2020, and led a SaaS start-up to be acquired by a leading-edge computing company in 2021. He currently advises and sits on the board of a marketing technology start-up.

In addition to his experience as an entrepreneur and leader, he earned his MBA, is currently a doctoral candidate for a DBA in Business Intelligence and teaches several courses and workshops as a member of the School of Marketing faculty at the Association of National Advertisers. He has served on the Virginia Tech Pamplin College of

Business Marketing Mentorship Advisory Board, the University of Richmond's CX Advisory Board, and was the founding chair of the American Advertising Federation's National Innovation Committee. Greg is Lean Six Sigma black belt certified, is an Agile Certified Coach (ICP-ACC) and holds a certification in Business Agility (ICP-BAF).

Greg has had multiple best-selling books, including his ten-part Agile Brand Guides series on marketing technology platforms and practices. His most recent book, the best-selling *House of the Customer* (2023) discusses the 1:1 personalized customer experience of the future, and how brands can organize the people, processes, and platforms that enable it. His award-winning podcast, *The Agile Brand with Greg Kihlström,* now in its sixth year with over 450 episodes and two million downloads, discusses brand strategy, marketing, and customer experience with some of the world's leading experts and leaders.

Greg is a contributing writer to Fast Company, Forbes, MarTech, CustomerThink, and CMSWire, and has been featured in publications such as *Advertising Age* and *The Washington Post*. Greg has been named a 2022 Top 10 Marketing and Customer Experience Thought Leader by Thinkers 360, was named one of ICMI's Top 25 CX Thought Leaders two years in a row, and a DC Inno 50 on Fire as a Washington DC trendsetter in marketing. He's also participated as a speaker at global industry events and has guest lectured at prominent universities and colleges.

RESOURCES

Many great resources are available for marketing technology professionals that can complement the ideas in this book. Included are a few related to The Agile Brand and Greg Kihlström's other work.

For other resources besides those in the following section, you can reach out to Greg Kihlström via LinkedIn: *https://www.linkedin.com/in/gregkihlstrom*

SUPPORTING LINKS

Agile Brand Guide Web site, featuring articles, a marketing technology wiki, as well as a product directory that includes AI-based tools: *https://www.agilebrandguide.com*

Agile Brand Guide podcast with Greg Kihlström: *https://www.gregkihlstrom.com/theagilebrandpodcast*

FOREWORD

The rapid evolution of AI between the end of 2022 and early 2023 will be marked as a watershed moment for the field. I was blown away by the speed and potential of the next generation of AI that came to market in between November of 2022 and the present. As the owner of a top-tier digital consulting and award-winning experience design firm, I couldn't help but feel both excited and confounded by its power, potential, and rapid evolution.

On one hand, I was eager to set up a consulting offering against it, develop a custom product, or at the very least, create our own tools, integrations, and processes. On the other hand, the agency was abuzz with discussions about ethics, diversity, correctness, singularity, job loss, and more. It felt like the proverbial paralysis/analysis limbo, stuck in a vicious cycle of potential versus risk mitigation.

That's why when my dear friend and co-futurist Greg approached me with the idea of developing a down-to-earth, pragmatic take on the topic of AI for marketers, my overall reaction was—"can't get it soon enough!"

This practical field guide provides a comprehensive overview of AI in marketing, covering everything from basic definitions and history to emerging opportunities. Greg's extensive research and experience in the field of marketing and AI have enabled him to provide real-world examples and practical advice on how to integrate and optimize AI into your marketing approach.

The book is divided into four parts, each addressing a different aspect of AI and marketing. Part I covers the fundamentals of AI in marketing, including machine learning and artificial intelligence. Part II delves into growth areas for marketing and AI, including generative AI and customer journey personalization. Part III goes into detail about how to use AI, particularly generative AI tools, to help in the marketing function in several ways. Part IV is all about integration and optimization, providing insights on when and where to invest in AI and how to prepare your team for an AI-driven marketing future.

I would like to emphasize that while AI is undoubtedly the future of marketing, it is also a rapidly evolving field. It's important to stay up to date with the latest trends and technologies, but it's equally important to make progress as the tools and systems evolve and ensure you can pivot when appropriate. Greg's book provides a solid foundation for understanding and harnessing the power of AI in marketing, but it's up to you to keep exploring and experimenting with new ways to integrate and optimize AI into your marketing approach.

I highly recommend this book to any marketing leader who wants to stay ahead of the curve and drive business growth through AI.

Carlos Manalo
Co-CEO and Cofounder
The Office of Experience

INTRODUCTION

The hype around technology trends seems continuous, with only the labels and the players changing from year to year. In no particular order: crypto, big data, social media, "the year of mobile," and the metaverse. Now, artificial intelligence (AI) is the center of the hype storm.

The world always seems to be "on the cusp" of some major transformative change that will usher in a new *era* of *something*. Those whose careers started with the advent of the first Internet boom in the late 1990s have seen their share of real and real-*seeming* (at the time) world-shattering breakthroughs. Some of those breakthroughs have truly lived up to their hype, and others are punchlines at worst and cautionary tales at best.

It's understandable to approach the topic of AI and its ability to transform marketing and business with a bit of trepidation. Be assured that some of the hype is inflated, yet some of the enthusiasm present in social feeds, inboxes, and across the news is justified.

With the adoption of artificial intelligence (AI) in all business areas more than doubling between 2017 and 2022, according to the McKinsey Global Survey on AI,[1] there is clearly momentum behind AI and that has only continued in the subsequent months. Although not everyone keeps up with the latest information on the topic, most people are aware of text-based technologies like OpenAI's GPT-4, Google's Gemini, and other large language models that power text-based products like ChatGPT or Gemini, as well as image-based ones like DALL-E or MidJourney.

As evidenced in subsequent chapters, it's more than likely readers have utilized at least some of many current usages of AI in marketing as well. Readers may be surprised to learn that if they've ever used a search engine, they have used AI as a consumer. The purpose of this guide is to provide an overview that marketing leaders and aspiring leaders can use to help guide their decisions, a street through the cloud of hype, and help in making informed decisions about the investment of time and money in the future.

WHY AI AND MARKETING?

In trying to address the concepts and trends that marketing leaders and aspiring leaders need to understand most, picking the topic of artificial intelligence was an obvious one. While AI is by no means a new thing to the marketing world, the recent hype brought by technologies like OpenAI's ChatGPT, and the nearly $50 billion raised by generative AI and AI-related start-ups in 2023[2] has caused a new wave of ideas, applications, and approaches to be considered by marketers and the companies they work for.

Because of this, it is time to tackle this topic in what will be a quick but ideally informative and inspirational read. There's no time to make a full history of AI and its impact on marketing, nor is it possible to cover all of the exciting recent developments. The goal, then, is to cover enough so that readers feel comfortable discussing this topic with their peers, exploring investments in the space and planning initiatives that incorporate some or all of the exciting methods that artificial intelligence can augment and enhance marketing efforts.

THIS BOOK IS BASED ON RESEARCH . . . AND EXPERIENCE

This book is an example of continually informed writing. The author has been privileged to work with several organizations of varying sizes (from

Fortune 50 to 1000, and even smaller on occasion) and assisted with some of the AI methods and tools described in this book. Additionally, the author has been tasked with researching and creating strategies for leading brands to potentially adopt and implement some of the newer additions to the pool of AI-based marketing tools.

The author is committed to being both a writer-researcher and a practitioner and wants his insights to be more than purely theoretical. His hope is that this makes the concepts on the page more actionable, insightful, and beneficial to the reader.

INTENDED AUDIENCE

This book is for marketing executives and professionals who want to understand how to implement Agile principles within their marketing to increase their effectiveness, including CMO and marketing leadership, marketing management, and other marketing team members.

Of those professionals, this book will be most useful for marketers with little understanding of Agile or may be tasked with exploring if Agile practices would be a good fit for their organization.

Also, this is an introduction, not an advanced user manual. Therefore, it is intended to be a short read and to quickly and easily give the reader a good understanding of the topic. However, to get more in-depth knowledge, more reading, training, and experience will be required.

WHAT THIS BOOK IS NOT

There is a brief mention of the history of AI and some related tools throughout the book, however this is not intended to be a full history of artificial intelligence or even a comprehensive documentation of when and how marketers have utilized AI throughout the last several decades.

Additionally, while several current and potential applications of artificial intelligence in marketing, customer experience, and related fields will be discussed, this book is not intended to be a guide on how to implement AI in marketing. Ideally, the reader will gain some additional insights into how it can be applied, however.

WHAT WILL BE COVERED

The author will share his knowledge and experience implementing artificial intelligence tools in a marketing environment. The book is divided into four main parts:

1. **Part 1:**

   The first part reviews some definitions, goes through a little history, and then explains why marketers should pay attention to AI in their work and plan for the future. The segment wraps up by reviewing some areas where artificial intelligence is already being used in marketing, and it may surprise some to see just how many areas there are.

2. **Part 2:**

   This part explores some of the areas where AI and marketing are the most exciting at the moment. These include:
   a. Generative AI, which includes technologies like ChatGPT, Gemini, and Claude, plus many new features within existing products and platforms
   b. Next best action and other predictive, propensity methods of personalizing the customer experience
   c. Team and workflow automation, which allows teams to accomplish more, get better results, and simply parse sets of data that humans alone can't accomplish

3. **Part 3:**

   The third part explains several practical examples of how to use generative AI tools to achieve goals such as creating effective content and analyzing marketing data.

4. **Part 4:**

   The final part discusses several ways marketers should start thinking about planning and adopting artificial intelligence tools, processes, and platforms and discuss what this means for how marketing is done. Additionally, two very important areas critical to the successful adoption of AI are discussed: understanding bias and ways to measure and optimize your efforts once you've begun.

Throughout this guide, the author has tried to strike a balance between giving an overview of AI in a marketing context and discussing practical examples that marketers should keep in mind when consideration of implementing it in their work is needed.

Further, the author most likely glossed over many areas where AI is currently used for two reasons: there are too many areas where some form of artificial intelligence (even if a very simple type) is used, and the purpose of this book is to explore some of the newer areas where there is still a lot of room for growth and development.

ADDITIONAL RESOURCES

There are some related resources, as mentioned within the chapters that follow, available on the following Web site: *https://gregkihlstrom.com/*

Feel free to contact the author if you have any questions or would like to be pointed in the right direction at the sites listed earlier or on LinkedIn at *https://www.linkedin.com/in/gregkihlstrom/*

NOTES

1 McKinsey & Company. "The State of AI in 2022—and a Half Decade in Review." December 6, 2022. Retrieved March 4, 2023 from https://www.mckinsey.com/capabilities/quantumblack/our-insights/the-state-of-ai-in-2022-and-a-half-decade-in-review

2 Metinko, Chris. "Artificial Buildup: AI Startups Were Hot in 2023, But This Year May Be Slightly Different." Crunchbase. January 9, 2024. Retrieved January 13, 2024 from https://news.crunchbase.com/ai/hot-startups-2023-openai-anthropic-forecast-2024/

Exploring AI and Marketing

This part will explore how artificial intelligence can help marketers get to know their customers better, do their work more easily, and achieve better results.

In this first part of the book, readers will go into a little background on some of the key terms related to AI. They will then go beyond the recent hype to look at some reasons marketers should pay attention to using artificial intelligence in their work.

The text explores some of the many areas where AI is already being utilized—there are quite a few—and then moves into the next section of the book to investigate some of the newer growth areas.

CHAPTER 1

A Brief History of AI

This volume will explore all the ways that artificial intelligence is helping marketers, and the many ways in which it will be helping more marketers in the future, but first it's important to understand some of the terms being used, and to take a short history lesson. Chief among the terms readers should understand are *artificial intelligence*, *machine learning*, and *algorithm*, although there are many others we will explore in the pages that follow.

The first term to go over is artificial intelligence (AI), which started in the 1940s, spurred on by World War II and its need for encryption, decryption, and other advanced mathematics. John Von Neumann and Alan Turing could be credited with being the founding fathers of the technology behind AI in the early 1950s, although they did not coin the term. According to the Council of Europe's History of Artificial Intelligence [COE23], the term "AI" is attributed to John McCarthy of MIT, who worked with Marvin Minsky of Carnegie-Mellon University to refine further what Minsky referred to as "the construction of computer programs that engage in tasks that are currently more satisfactorily performed by human beings because they require high-level mental processes such as: perceptual learning, memory organization and critical reasoning."[1]

AI's growth has been accelerated by the same technologies that have spawned countless other advances, such as smaller processors, the ability to store greater amounts of data, and, more recently, the ability of computer graphics card processors to accelerate the calculation of learning algorithms, which helped give rise to what is known as *machine learning* (ML). The term itself was coined in 1952 by Arthur Samuel, a computer scientist at IBM. According to Pandio's history of machine learning [PAN23], while machine learning got off to a slightly slower start in terms of development than more traditional AI, IBM's creation of the Deep Blue supercomputer (see Figure 1.1), which famously beat chess champion Garry Kasparov at the game in 1997, brought machine learning to the forefront.[2]

FIGURE 1.1. An IBM Deep Blue computer, similar to the one that beat chess champion Garry Kasparov in 1997 (Courtesy Wikimedia Commons). *https://commons.wikimedia.org/wiki/Category:Deep_Blue#/media/ File:IBM_rs6000_SP_-_Deep_Blue.jpg*

WHAT'S THE DIFFERENCE BETWEEN MACHINE LEARNING AND ARTIFICIAL INTELLIGENCE?

AI and ML, or machine learning, are often used synonymously, though they are not exactly the same. Rather, machine learning is a subset of artificial intelligence.

In layman's terms, artificial intelligence can be defined as using machines (most often computers) to mimic human intelligence to do work or otherwise perform tasks. These tasks are most often heavily scripted—as in, there is a well-defined series of tasks that are performed in a specific order—and while the outcomes can vary greatly depending on the inputs, despite the name, they are not terribly "intelligent" in the way we often think of human's ability to be creative and adaptive to new or unforeseen circumstances. For those areas, machine learning can be more helpful.

Machine learning, or ML, can be thought of as a subset or type of AI. Rather than being restricted to utilizing the same "recipe" (or algorithm, which we'll define in a minute) for every action, they utilize models that can learn from data patterns without additional input from humans. ML is incredibly helpful in the age of big data, where data warehouses, data lakes, and the continually growing stores of data prove daunting for human-created AI algorithms to parse.

WHAT ABOUT ALGORITHMS?

You have undoubtedly heard the term *algorithm* from time to time in everything from a critique of the quality of Google versus Bing's search algorithm or any other such examples. But what is an algorithm?

According to an article by Marek Kowalkiewicz [KOWALKIEWICZ19], the name originates from the name of Muhammad ibn Mūsā al'Khwārizmī, a ninth-century Persian mathematician whose Latinized name, Algoritmi, meant "the decimal number system.[3]" The Oxford Dictionary [OXF23] states that algorithms, as a more modern concept, became more commonly known in English in the nineteenth century[4] and grew in popularity, particularly since the 1950s, with the advent of the availability of commercial computers.

But, to be more specific to the topics in this book, an *algorithm* is a step-by-step procedure for solving a problem or achieving a goal. It is a well-defined process that takes some input and produces a corresponding output.

An algorithm can be as simple as the formula in a cell in an Excel sheet or a Macro in Word, a series of tasks in a program like IFTTT (which stands for "if this then that"), or it can be much more complex and have many steps and variables contained within it. But chances are you have created an algorithm of your own, if not worked with countless algorithms in your career so far.

CONCLUSION

So, what does all of this history of artificial intelligence have to do with marketing, particularly modern marketing? In the next chapter, we will explore the relevance to marketers of all kinds and why AI is not only here to stay but to grow in its relevance to marketing, advertising, and the overall customer experience.

NOTES

1   [COE23] Council of Europe. "History of Artificial Intelligence." Retrieved March 4, 2023 from https://www.coe.int/en/web/artificial-intelligence/history-of-ai.

2   [PAN23] Pandio. "A Brief History of Machine Learning." Retrieved March 4, 2023 from https://pandio.com/when-was-machine-learning-invented/.

3   [KOWALKIEWICZ19] Kowalkiewicz, Marek. "How did we get here? The story of algorithms." *Medium*. October 10, 2019. Retrieved March 4, 2023 from https://towardsdatascience.com/how-did-we-get-here-the-story-of-algorithms-9ee186ba2a07.

4   [OXF23] Oxford English Dictionary. Retrieved March 4, 2023 from www.oed.com/view/Entry/4959.

CHAPTER 2

UNDERSTANDING *AI* AND *MARKETING*

As a marketer, staying ahead of the competition means understanding and incorporating the latest technology into existing methods and ensuring they are performing well. One such area that is essential for modern marketers to understand is artificial intelligence. In spite of the recent hype, which just might be magnifying the state of things from time to time, AI has already been profoundly impacting businesses worldwide, transforming how we do marketing. With its ability to automate processes, analyze data at scale, and uncover key insights, AI presents tremendous opportunities for marketers to reach customers more efficiently than ever before.

This chapter will explore why understanding AI is so important for marketers today—from providing more personalized customer experiences to driving efficiency in their campaigns. The following text looks at three reasons marketers should pay attention to how artificial intelligence can and will impact their work.

AI IS GREAT AT WHAT HUMANS ARE NOT

Although you may excel at work that involves more strategic thinking, there can be the occasional satisfaction from working on a very repetitive task like filling out a spreadsheet or something that doesn't require a lot of creative thinking. Despite that temporary need to "clear one's head" while remaining somewhat productive, most people wouldn't want to do that repetitive work all day for hours without rest.

While many humans are in jobs that require a great deal of repetition, in many cases, the right machine can sustainably do the same or similar tasks longer and with fewer errors.

Machines, or AI, in this case, thrive when doing repetitive tasks. If they had feelings, they would *love* them and prefer them over poorly defined tasks that require creativity and rapid adaptivity. Thus, AI is great at what humans are not when it comes to repetition and other tasks that don't require strategic thinking, creativity, rapid improvisation, and other very human strengths.

Conversely, when it comes to parsing large sets of data and finding patterns within them, this is another area where humans aren't as good. Whether it is the difficulty of calculating large numbers, the biases that humans can introduce based on the first or last thing they see (or, according to Jeff Desjardins [DESJARDINS21], the other 180-plus cognitive biases that exist in humans[1]), or other limitations of the human brain, humans simply don't do well when it comes to an understanding and interpreting huge data sets. Again, this is where AI is a huge help and where machine learning can adapt its capabilities to make sense of all the information.

While humans have adapted to a wide range of types of work over the years, it doesn't mean they are best suited for all of it. Instead, AI and machines can be great team members that pick up the slack when repetitive tasks or overwhelming data sets are part of the equation.

AI CAN SERVE AS A GREAT STARTING POINT

Even in some areas where humans are better at tasks than machines, AI can serve as a great jumping-off point. For instance, if a marketing team is tasked with creating five blogs in a short time, it can be quite daunting to think about picking a topic, researching, getting started on writing, revising, and completing.

For instance, using a local copy of Llama 2, the following prompt was submitted:

```
Please provide me with (ten) blog topic ideas that
would appeal to marketing leaders who are learning about
the impact of AI on their profession
```

It returned the following:

Sure, here are ten blog topic ideas that would appeal to marketing leaders who are learning about the impact of AI on their profession:

1. *"The Future of Marketing: How AI is Revolutionizing the Industry"—This post could explore the current and potential applications of AI in marketing, including personalization, automation, and predictive analytics.*

2. *"AI-Powered Customer Insights: What Marketers Need to Know"—This article could delve into how AI can help marketers better understand their customers, from demographic data to sentiment analysis and beyond.*

3. *"The Role of AI in Personalized Marketing Strategies" - This post could discuss the ways in which AI can be used to create personalized experiences for customers, including dynamic content and messaging.*

4. *"How AI is Changing the Way We Measure Marketing Success"—This article could explore how AI-powered analytics tools are enabling marketers to measure the effectiveness of their campaigns in real time, and make data-driven decisions as a result.*

5. *"The Ethics of AI in Marketing: Balancing Technology with Human Values"—This post could examine the ethical considerations surrounding the use of AI in marketing, including issues related to privacy, bias, and transparency.*

Each of these topics offers a wealth of opportunities for exploration and analysis, and could provide valuable insights for marketing leaders seeking to understand the impact of AI on their profession.

As one can see, none of these topic suggestions are flawless, and each would need work to make them more compelling and interesting, but any of them could be improved and made into a relevant and informative post with some additional *human* creativity added to them.

With the help of AI, particularly some of the generative tools discussed in the next section of the book, portions of this can be made easier. Humans are great when it comes to creative ideas, so maybe a team can brainstorm (still a very human activity) five topic ideas. But then, the team can take those ideas and get an AI-based tool to provide some starting points, whether bullet points, an opening paragraph or two, or even a rough draft that might need some heavy editing to be on brand and on target.

Still, in this case, AI is incredibly helpful as a starting point and can help a team get over writer's block while still providing the creativity and flexibility that humans are still required to contribute.

This is yet another example of how artificial intelligence is greatest when it can be thought of as an *augmentation*, not a *replacement*, of humans and the work of people.

AI ISN'T SCARY; IT'S JOB SECURITY

Finally, let's be pragmatic about the future. Artificial intelligence, machine learning, and the associated tools and approaches are here to stay. More likely, they will continue to grow at an increasing rate for at least a while until there might be a plateau where humans reach an equilibrium between what machines can do and what humans are still required to oversee, design, and manage.

Because of this, it is important to embrace the idea that AI will continually be a part of work as a marketer and people should try to have an open mind about it. That does not mean blindly following trends, adopting things that don't make sense, or generating worse quality or results. But it does mean that job security may depend on learning and adopting the types of AI-based tools, platforms, and methods that can bring value to an organization.

CONCLUSION

Even at a high level, there are many reasons marketers should pay attention to AI. Before exploring some of the newer and growing interests, the next chapter explores some areas in which AI is already incorporated into some of the marketing activities teams are performing.

NOTE

1   [DESJARDINS21] Desjardins, Jeff. "24 Cognitive Biases That Are Warping Your Perception of Reality." Visual Capitalist. November 26, 2021. Retrieved March 4, 2023 from https://www.visualcapitalist.com/24-cognitive-biases-warping-reality/.

THE CURRENT USE OF AI IN MARKETING

With all of the hype surrounding artificial intelligence-based technologies like ChatGPT and other generative AI tools, it may be easy to forget that AI has been around for decades, and its usage in marketing is already quite extensive.

Before exploring some of AI's newer and more advanced uses in marketing and related fields, readers can explore some of the many ways AI is already being applied. Some of the uses may be familiar, and the following briefly demonstrate the breadth of use and highlights some areas where AI may be underappreciated.

SEARCH

Let's start with what may be the most commonly used method of AI incorporated with marketing: search. If a person performs one of the 8.5 billion searches a day using Google[1] (Figure 3.1), they have used both of these artificial intelligence applications as a consumer. You can learn more about related search statistics in Maryam Mohsin's article for Oberlo.com [MOSHIN23].

The most commonly known usage of AI in search is what many refer to as the *algorithm*. While we discussed the definition of an algorithm earlier, it's important to note that Google's algorithm, for instance, is not just a single thing. It is actually a series of algorithms and AI technologies working with one another to determine relevance and context, among other things.

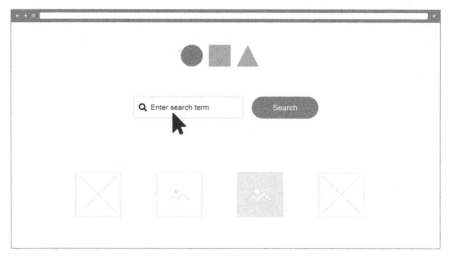

FIGURE 3.1. Anyone who has performed a search on a Web site or search engine has interacted with AI in the form of an algorithm.

Search utilizes AI in several additional ways, including the way a search engine ranks Web pages and other content by authority on a particular subject matter by using natural language processing (NLP) to understand the syntax and context of search results (e.g., is it a question that needs to be answered?), as well as to use machine learning to improve the results continually. This is just a high-level view of things, however. Much more goes into a Google (or any other) search.

Additionally, image search has come a long way, and image recognition is a method that heavily relies on AI and, specifically, machine learning.

Marketers are utilizing search in a few ways. First, there is search engine optimization (SEO), which allows brands to show up organically or naturally within Google, Bing, or other search results by creating relevant content that ranks highly. Then, there is the ability to purchase paid advertising on those search platforms when users search relevant terms.

Additionally, search is utilized on most Web sites to search content within the site itself using platforms like Algolia (which powers everything from Web site searches to searches on platforms like Playstation), among others. While not all visitors to a Web site will gravitate toward "search" as their preferred method of navigation, there are some to whom this is the first thing they do. Thus, optimizing a Web site for both external searches from Google and others and optimizing it for internal searches are both important considerations.

Of course, with the steep rise of generative AI adoption, search engines have already been incorporating it in meaningful ways, starting with Microsoft Bing and Edge's adoption of OpenAI's GPT 3.5 as early as February of 2023 [MEHDI23],[2] and with Google following shortly after with its release of Bard, now known as Gemini.

How Search Is Used

- **Search across the Web** via text, images, videos, shopping, and more on platforms such as Google, Microsoft Bing, and others

- **Web site searches** within a specific online property or set of properties

- **Voice search** utilizing Alexa (Amazon), Siri (Apple), or others

RECOMMENDATIONS, PERSONALIZATION, AND PREDICTION

Those among the 170 million-plus people a year in the United States who have bought a product on Amazon [BRADLEY23][3] have undoubtedly seen one of the first and most sophisticated recommendation engines. At the present time, recommendations technology is much more readily available and can take a very simplified or more complex approach than the original one used by Amazon since the 1990s.

Some simple examples of recommendations include recommending content or products based on similar purchases or click-through behavior, as seen in Figure 3.2. More complex recommendations can combine several factors using more complex algorithms and machine learning to determine a consumer's propensity to need or want a specific product or service.

Similarly, personalization can be very simple or take on more complex forms and has been used in some capacity nearly since the advent of the Web. Simple personalization could be more accurately termed "substitution." An example will be inserting one's first name in an email subject line or welcoming the user by name to a Web site if they are already logged in.

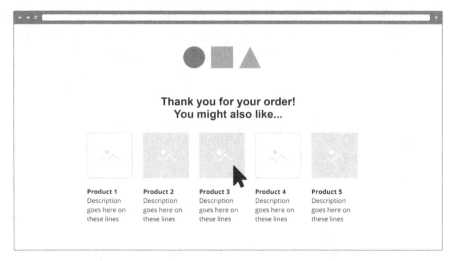

FIGURE 3.2. Product recommendations based on similar characteristics, past searches, or other behavior are a common example of AI in e-commerce.

More complex personalization examples are driven by behavioral activity or a combination of calculations that generate a propensity to act in a certain way, be ready to buy a certain product or service, or something similar.

Additionally, building on personalization and recommendations is the ability to predict what a customer will do. In some cases, there isn't a lot of distinction between what a recommendation and a prediction may be. The latter is most often associated with a quantifiable score such as propensity to buy or lead scoring.

How Recommendations and Personalization Are Used

- **Product recommendations** based on a specific customer's preferences

- **Other customers who bought this product** also bought *this other product*

- **Personalized content** including both substitution of simple parameters (like a first name), as well as more complex items like purchase history or other behaviors

- **Personalized offers and deals**, including dynamic pricing

- **Ad retargeting** across search and display based on Web site visits, email opens and clicks, or other behavior

- **Marketing automation**, which is commonly used for things like email marketing workflows and other predetermined sequences of communications based on a user action

- **Predictive analytics**, which we also will explore in more depth in the next section

- **Programmatic ad buying**

- **Propensity modeling and lead scoring**

WORKFLOW AUTOMATION

Workflow and task automation is an area we will come back to in our next section as well because this is such a big area of opportunity for marketers to embrace in the years ahead.

Currently, what is known as robotic process automation (RPA) is the most prevalent aspect of workflow automation. This can be described as automation software intended to augment or replace repetitive tasks that humans are currently doing. So, instead of people doing multistep tasks that involve data entry, navigating between systems, identifying and extracting data, and other time-consuming work, these RPA systems can take over most, if not all, of the work. It has turned out to be quite popular in the world of business. In fact, McKinsey's 2022 Global Survey on AI [MCKINSEY22] showed that RPA was the most used AI capability out of more than a dozen.[4]

While RPA may bring to mind visuals of highly complex tasks that a series of "robots" are needed to perform, this type of automation can be used for very simple tasks as well. Think of anything a team does regularly that does not require complex interpretations or for which the requirements do not vastly change each day, week, or month.

How RPA Is Used

- **Robotic Process Automation (RPA)** of marketing tasks

- **Batch processing** of customer data and other marketing information

- **Automated transfer** of files and other information

- **Automated generation** of standardized reports

CONCLUSION

Readers have most likely seen some, if not all, of these applications of AI and marketing in action in work situations. As mentioned at the beginning of this chapter, there are not only several methods that artificial intelligence has found its way into work; many are very much commonplace in today's marketing environments.

It is important to mention these to show that not only are there newer and exciting uses for AI in marketing but also to demonstrate that artificial intelligence and marketing is by no means a new or novel idea.

This chapter explored some of the common methods for which AI is used, and subsequent text explores some areas where there is a lot of growth and where new developments are particularly exciting and important for marketers to understand.

NOTES

1   [MOSHIN23] Mohsin, Maryam. "10 Google Search Statistics You Need to Know in 2023." Oberlo.com. January 13, 2023. Retrieved March 4, 2023 from https://www.oberlo.com/blog/google-search-statistics.

2   [MEHDI23] Mehdi, Yusuf. "Reinventing Search with a New AI-Powered Microsoft Bing and Edge, Your Copilot for the Web." Official Microsoft blog. *Microsoft.* February 7, 2023. Retrieved April 4, 2024 from https://blogs.microsoft.com/blog/2023/02/07/reinventing-search-with-a-new-ai-powered-microsoft-bing-and-edge-your-copilot-for-the-web/.

3   [BRADLEY23] Bradley T. "Amazon Statistics: Key Numbers and Fun Facts." AMZ Scout. Retrieved March 4, 2023 from https://amzscout.net/blog/amazon-statistics/#:~:text=Number%20of%20Amazon%20Users,-How%20many%20people&text=It%20is%20estimated%20that%20the,on%20Amazon%20in%20the%20US.

4   [MCKINSEY22] McKinsey. "The State of AI in 2022—and a Half Decade in Review." December 6, 2022. Retrieved March 4, 2023 from https://www.mckinsey.com/capabilities/quantumblack/our-insights/the-state-of-ai-in-2022-and-a-half-decade-in-review.

PART II

GROWTH AREAS FOR MARKETING AND AI

Now that readers have reviewed where AI is *already* being used effectively in marketing, it's time to explore some of the areas that are, in some cases, newer and, in all cases, the most exciting and actively growing in their sophistication. That is important to highlight because, in some sense, there is nothing truly new about these applications of artificial intelligence. Rather, they are all some type of evolution of what has preceded them. Some of what is new are the enthusiasm behind them and the sheer ubiquity of how AI is being put at the forefront of marketing applications. In other words, instead of simply touting "AI" or "algorithms" in the promotional copy about a product, they are giving marketers a more direct interface to interact with the AI components of products.

Perhaps one of the most direct and talked-about versions of this is the ChatGPT interface, which exists as a conversation between the user and the AI model. While ChatGPT or other similar tools are not specifically made for marketers, there are several tools discussed in this section whose primary audience is marketers.

Before the discussion surrounding all of the new things that AI brings to the marketing world continues, the sheer amount of hype surrounding AI and marketing, from late 2022 to today, should be noted.

FIRST, LET'S ADDRESS THE HYPE

Some of this hype is optimistic and points to a wealth of opportunities, at least the abundant potential of how AI can help organizations address challenges and opportunities via increased productivity, human augmentation, a vast ability to crunch numbers and statistics, and many more things. If one has been paying attention to the hype cycles, they have surely seen this for any number of technology-related phenomena from social media to blockchain, to big data, or to the endless heralding that each new year would be the "year of mobile," until that finally came to be once Apple released the iPhone on June 29, 2007 [MONTGOMERY22].[1]

Likewise, some of this hype is also a mixture of pessimism and doomsday predictions and the end of everything currently known and loved. Although that statement may be a bit dramatic, when people read stories, such as the one in Steve Mollman's article for *Fortune* [MOLLMAN23] about ChatGPT passing a Wharton MBA exam[2] causing instructors to have to rethink the way they structure their curriculum [HUANG23][3] or enabling the creation of polymorphic Malware that, according to Allesandro Mascellino's article in *Info Security Magazine* [MASCELLINO23], can "easily evade security products and make mitigation cumbersome with very little effort or investment by the adversary,"[4] it may seem as the death knell for current civilization.

The reality of it all is much more likely somewhere balanced between the two. After all, according to an article by Chloe Xiang for Vice [XIANG23], as early as January of 2023, Edward Tian, a Princeton student and journalist, created GPTZero, a tool that helps detect text written by the popular ChatGPT tool.[5] The takeaway here is that, as quickly as AI tools and technology may be advancing and able to "fool" humans into thinking that information is human-generated rather than AI-generated, tools are being created to assist us in knowing the difference between the two. Perhaps ironically, these tools will likely all use their form of artificial intelligence to do so. It's important to note, however, that while there is potential for real and imagined risk, there is also the possibility for greater things to be created by real people with the augmentation of AI tools.

While an entire book could be written about the dangers of AI, with an acknowledgment of some of the dangers of bias in the next section, the focus of the rest of this book on the opportunities and optimistic view the artificial intelligence will be able to help marketers to greater things; people and AI working together in a way that benefits our customers and our brands.

NOW, THE REAL OPPORTUNITY

As discussed, there is a real, tangible opportunity for AI and marketing to do some amazing things together, and, as we saw in the last section, that is already true. But, despite many new companies entering the market, and current platforms rolling out generative AI and other related features on a weekly, if not daily basis, we are really only scratching the surface at the moment, with a lot of investment and focus across many sectors on AI tools. There will be a lot of change and growth in this area in the months and years ahead.

This ranges from improvements in the ability of artificial intelligence to understand and write domain-specific copy for all types of channels and mediums, from Web site copy, to emails, advertisements, and other sales materials, and more.

Additionally, the quality of results seems to be improving by an order of magnitude nearly every six months, so expect massive change in a short amount of time.

In this part of the book, the author will discuss four of the most promising areas where artificial intelligence is transforming marketing, as illustrated in Figure PII.1. Other areas of business and what this means for the way teams work will also be discussed.

These four areas include:

1. generative AI, which includes applications like ChatGPT or image generation tools that allow marketers to create written and image-based content more quickly and easily than ever before

2. personalized customer experience, which uses predictive modeling and journey orchestration to anticipate and deliver customized customer experience

3. team and workflow automation, which introduces AI elements to existing teams, and augments what human teams are able to do

4. measurement and optimization, which use predictive analytics, dynamic audience segmentation, and other capabilities to help us understand the effectiveness of our marketing work

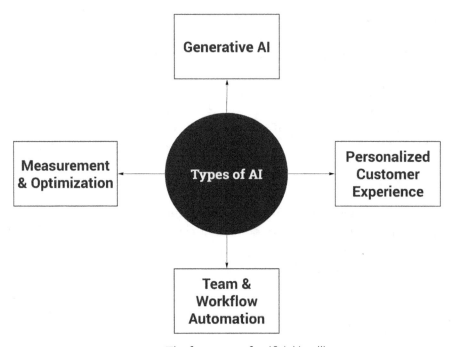

FIGURE PII.1. The four types of artificial intelligence.

NOTES

1 [MONTGOMERY22] Montgomery, April, and Ken Mingis. "The Evolution of Apple's iPhone." Computerworld. September 14, 2022. Retrieved March 4, 2023 from https://www.computerworld.com/article/2604020/the-evolution-of-apples-iphone.html.

2 [MOLLMAN23] Mollman, Steve. "ChatGPT Passed a Wharton MBA Exam and It's Still in Its Infancy. One Professor is Sounding the Alarm." *Fortune Magazine.* January 21, 2023. Retrieved March 4, 2023 from https://fortune.com/2023/01/21/chatgpt-passed-wharton-mba-exam-one-professor-is-sounding-alarm-artificial-intelligence/.

3   [HUANG23] Huang, Kalley. "Alarmed by A.I. Chatbots, Universities Start Revamping How They Teach." *The New York Times*. January 16, 2023. Retrieved March 4, 2023 from https://www.nytimes.com/2023/01/16/technology/chatgpt-artificial-intelligence-universities.html.

4   [MASCELLINO23] Mascellino, Allesandro. "ChatGPT Creates Polymorphi Malware." *Infosecurity Magazine*. January 18, 2023. Retrieved March 4, 2023 from https://www.infosecurity-magazine.com/news/chatgpt-creates-polymorphic-malware/.

5   [XIANG23] Xiang, Chloe. "A CompSci Student Built an App That Can Detect ChatGPT-Generated Text." Vice. January 6, 2023. Retrieved March 4, 2023 from https://www.vice.com/en/article/3admg8/a-compsci-student-built-an-app-that-can-detect-chatgpt-generated-text.

CHAPTER 4

GENERATIVE AI

We will start our exploration of the biggest growth areas of AI for marketers with what is arguably the most significant of the lot: generative AI. With large language models from OpenAI (GPT-4), Google (Gemini), and Meta (Llama), and tools like ChatGPT, Claude, Gemini, MidJourney, Stable Diffusion, and others fitting in this category, there is seemingly continual talk about it.

Generative AI is a technology that has gained widespread popularity over the past few years. It is a form of artificial intelligence that uses algorithms to generate new content, such as text, images, and even music. Generative AI tools can be used in a wide range of applications, including creative projects, data analysis, and other areas of marketing where text, images, or both are needed to achieve the desired results.

The primary role of generative AI is to create new content indistinguishable from that created by humans. This is achieved using machine learning algorithms to analyze existing data and generate new content based on patterns identified in that data. The result is a tool that can create unique and high-quality content.

The use of generative AI tools is not without its challenges. Users of these applications may face issues such as limited customization options, difficulty interpreting the output, and ethical concerns regarding using AI-generated content. This chapter will explore some of the most popular generative AI tools on the market, including ChatGPT, DALL-E, MidJourney, Stable Diffusion, and others.

AI-BASED PLATFORMS

Two categories of platforms will be explored: newer, AI-based platforms, as well as existing platforms that have added generative AI features. Examined first are the features and benefits of each tool and the challenges that users may face when using them.

Text Generation

The information starts with the category that may be most familiar to the majority of people. Text generation platforms, including the first one listed here (ChatGPT) are what seemingly kicked off the recent generative AI frenzy. While most generative AI platforms respond to text-based prompts, their output is where they can vary greatly. To reduce confusion, when we mention "text generation" platforms, these are platforms that *generate* text-based responses and output. Their inputs are likely text as well, but so are many of the others we will explore, so keep in mind that we are focused on the types of content that a user will generate when exploring these categories.

OpenAI ChatGPT

ChatGPT is one of the most popular generative AI tools on the market today, with over 60% of the overall traffic received from all AI tools, according to a recent Writerbuddy study [SARKAR24] on the most visited AI tools from September 2022 to August 2023.[1] It is described by Eliot Lance in his *Forbes* article [ELIOT23] as "a general-purpose AI interactive conversational-oriented system,"[2] with the GPT standing for generative pre-trained transformer. It is a language model developed by OpenAI that can generate human-like responses to text prompts. ChatGPT is particularly popular in the chatbot industry, where it is used to create chatbots that can interact with users naturally and intuitively. Released for testing to the general public in November 2022, it's already considered the best AI chatbot ever and, prior to Meta's Threads launch in mid-2023 (which subsequently dethroned ChatGPT [PORTER23][3]), was the fastest-growing platform in history, with a million people signed up to use it in just five days [MCKINSEY23],[4] and it has surpassed one hundred million users within the first two months of launch with more than thirteen million daily visitors as of January 2023 [RUBY23].[5] While the rate of growth did not continue at the same pace throughout 2023, as of August 2023, the number of worldwide unique visitors did increase to 180.5 million [TONG23].[6]

One of the key benefits of a generative AI tool like ChatGPT is its ability to generate specialized responses tailored to the user's specific needs (as shown in Figure 4.1), as inputs follow an easy-to-use chat interface and allow for very specific instructions. For example, a chatbot built using ChatGPT can be programmed to respond to specific keywords or phrases, making it easier for users to find the information they need. Simply type in the desired phrase, such as "Write me an 800-word blog post for marketers about the importance of predictive analytics and target it toward companies based in APAC," and an applicable response will be generated. One could just as easily request something in a different format, such as a book chapter, the beginning of a white paper, a novel, or even a television script.

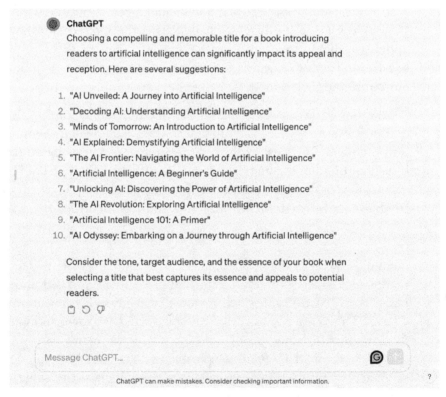

FIGURE 4.1. The results of a ChatGPT prompt asking "provide ideas for book titles for a book introducing readers to artificial intelligence."

Another benefit of ChatGPT is its ability to learn and improve over time. The tool uses machine learning algorithms to analyze user interactions and generate more accurate and relevant responses. This means that chatbots built using ChatGPT can become more effective over time as they learn from user feedback and interactions. More discussion in terms of potential bias will follow. ChatGPT and other generative AI's effectiveness rely on their ability to access accurate and diverse information so that they can take a holistic approach to provide answers.

That said, major integrations and investments, such as Microsoft's $10 billion investment (which followed its initial investment of $1 billion in July 2019) and its work to integrate ChatGPT with its Bing search engine, seem to promise that it will continue to become more effective and advanced over time. For more on this you can refer to Ashley Capoot's article for CNBC [CAPOOT23].[7]

It is clear that there are also some challenges associated with using ChatGPT. One of the biggest challenges is the limited customization options available to users. While ChatGPT can generate responses based on specific keywords or phrases, users may find it difficult to customize the tool to meet their specific needs.

Another challenge with ChatGPT is the difficulty in interpreting the output for accuracy and the original sources from which the information is generated. Because the tool generates responses based on patterns identified in existing data, it can be difficult to understand how it arrived at a particular response. This can make it difficult for users to troubleshoot issues or identify areas for improvement.

Google Gemini

Gemini is Google's conversational AI tool, based on its large language model, also called Gemini. It launched in February of 2023 under the name Bard [ALBA23],[8] which meant that it missed the peak hype of ChatGPT's release weeks earlier, the platform has grown and matured over the months since. As of February 2024, the name Bard was discarded in favor of Gemini, which means that both Google's conversational AI tool and its large language model share the same name [PIERCE24].[9]

While Gemini functions in a similar manner as rival ChatGPT, using a chat interface to receive prompts and questions, Google's platform has a few unique features, based on its close ties to other Google products. Thus, Gemini can access data and content from other Google apps and services such as Maps, Gmail, Docs, Drive, Flights, and YouTube. This means that users of Gemini can apply this tool to their own content if desired.

What this also means is that a key difference between Gemini and ChatGPT are that the latter's responses are based on data made available up to April 2023, while Google's Gemini, according to Andy Patrizio's article in TechTarget [PATRIZIO24] has the capability to use current, up-to-the-minute data.[10]

Anthropic Claude

A third text-based generative AI platform is Anthropic's Claude, formed by Daniela and Dario Amodei, siblings who are also former senior members of OpenAI [VICTOR23].[11]

Claude operates similarly to ChatGPT in that it has a text-based chat interface, so it allows users to enter in natural language questions and prompts. Also similar to ChatGPT, it doesn't search the Web to form answers to your questions and prompts, though it is capable of understanding text at a given URL that it is pointed to within a prompt. Claude also understands programming languages (as well as ten human languages) so it can provide flexibility in the inputs it receives.

Image Generation

The next category of platforms uses text-based inputs (and potentially other inputs) to produce static images. These tools range from ones that can generate any image a user can imagine—and describe with a text prompt—to those with a very focused use case.

Open AI DALL-E

DALL-E is a generative AI tool developed by OpenAI that can generate unique images from text prompts. The tool uses a combination of machine learning algorithms and neural networks to analyze text and generate corresponding images. DALL-E is particularly popular in the creative industry, used to generate new and innovative designs.

One of the key benefits of DALL-E is its ability to create images that are both unique and high-quality. The tool uses a deep learning algorithm to analyze existing data and generate images similar in style and composition to those created by human designers. This means that designers can use DALL-E to create new and innovative designs that would be difficult to create using traditional design tools.

Another benefit of DALL-E is its ability to generate images quickly and efficiently based on natural language requests, similar to how ChatGPT does the same for text-based responses, as illustrated in Figure 4.2, where the following prompt was given: "an expressive oil painting of a basketball player dunking, depicted as an explosion of a nebula." The tool uses a neural network to analyze text and generate corresponding images in real-time. For example, it could be used by artists and designers to quickly generate ideas for projects without having to manually create each image. Additionally, it could also be used to generate Web site content, such as product photos or advertising banners, automatically based on user input.

FIGURE 4.2. A DALL-E 2-generated image based on the prompt "an expressive oil painting of a basketball player dunking, depicted as an explosion of a nebula."

The challenges of DALL-E, along with the other tools listed here, come with the inability to determine source images in some cases and in preventing them from using copyrighted images. We'll talk about that a little bit more when we talk about Stable Diffusion.

Stable Diffusion and Midjourney

Stable Diffusion and Midjourney are two generative AI tools that use a deep learning model to generate images in various styles, including abstract, impressionist, expressionist, and many others. The tools can also generate unique and original images, which is a significant benefit for artists and designers who would otherwise have to create those from original drawings, 3D renderings, or other means.

One of the benefits of using a tool like Stable Diffusion or Midjourney is their ability to generate high-quality images that are indistinguishable from human-produced images. They also have a user-friendly interface allowing users to interact with the tool easily. Alternatively, one of the challenges of using these image generation tools is that it can be difficult to determine the source of the imagery and whether those images are copyrighted.

For instance, in January 2023, three artists, Sarah Andersen, Kelly McKernan, and Karla Ortiz, filed a lawsuit for copyright infringement against Stability AI, Midjourney, and DeviantArt, claiming that these companies have infringed the rights of countless artists, as their AI tools were trained on images used without the consent of the creators of those images [VINCENT23].[12]

Secta

As an example of a more focused type of image generation that mostly does not rely on text prompts, Secta.ai is a generative AI headshot generator. It takes existing photos (about twenty-five to thirty are recommended) and, based on those and a few selections asking questions about the background setting, facial expression, etc. it generates a series of new headshots of the individual that meet the desired requirements of backgrounds, settings, and also allows a user to refine those results to create higher resolution versions, change the coloring, and even change the facial expression.

Unlike some of the other image examples, this is Secta's sole function, thus it is able to produce a wide variety of types of headshots, though if you want a great photo of the front of your house, you would need to look elsewhere.

Video Generation

If there are text generators and image generators, it stands to reason that there would also be video generation, and that is the case. Though it is important to understand that generating a video requires a considerably larger amount of processing power. This is due in part to the fact that a video is essentially a series of still images, so the power to generate one high-definition image frame at 1920x1080 pixels needs to be multiplied by the frame rate (typically between twenty-four to thirty frames per second) as well as the length of the desired video. This means that a thirty-second video at twenty-four frames per second is the equivalent of generating 720 static images. There are technologies in place that are aiming to accelerate this and even change how we think about generating video, which we'll briefly discuss in relation to OpenAI's Sora, but the processor-intensive nature of generating video still poses limitations on what can be created.

Capcut

So far, we've only discussed text and image generators, though Capcut is a popular generative AI *video* generator that offers video manipulation to remove backgrounds, resize videos, and offers speech to text (for captioning), text to speech, and several other key features for marketers that create video content.

Similar to other video generation platforms like GAN.ai, Veed.io, and others, Capcut has both a Web and mobile app interface and focuses on ease of use. Though they are easy to use, as with all of the platforms at this current stage, there can be some limitations in how customized they can be, often relying on templatized areas of the screen and other approaches to make generation of the videos less processor-intensive.

Synthesia

Another popular video platform that utilizes generative AI is Synthesia that claims to turn text-based prompts into video utilizing AI avatars within minutes and able to handle over 130 languages. This ease of use has the potential to make creating customized generative AI videos as easy as creating a PowerPoint deck.

This can be helpful for sales teams that want something that feels more personalized, or for marketing or customer service teams for which a dry PowerPoint deck may not be well received by a future or current customer.

OpenAI Sora

As of the writing of this book, OpenAI's Sora is not available to the public at large, but its initial preview has been viewed as somewhat of a game changer in its ability to generate full-motion, high-definition video that is as photorealistic and/or imaginative as the static images created by DALL-E or Midjourney.

In a research paper by some of the creators of Sora, the AI approach is described as using visual "patches" that are able to approximate full-motion portions of a piece of video, which is ultimately a portion of an animated *world* that the generated video captures.[13]

Marketing Assistants

The next category of generative AI platforms offers more than one type of output, often from a single prompt. They have the capability to create text output, image output, and even help with planning and execution of marketing campaigns and initiatives.

Tailwind

Tailwind is an all-in-one AI-based marketing tool that describes itself as a marketing "copilot," offering help with writing for multiple channels as well as image generation to support marketing campaigns. Additionally, it offers the ability to create a marketing plan with scheduling and recommendations of when to approach different marketing tactics to achieve success.

Jasper

Similarly, Jasper is another tool targeted specifically at marketers, which, in its homepage copy [JASPER23], touts its ability to help marketers write content more quickly, translate it into different languages, and generate new ideas. Reading between the lines, they are clearly not saying that their AI is a replacement for human writers, but more, as we've discussed previously, as an augmentation to existing marketing teams.[14]

SwellAI

As an example of a more focused tool, SwellAI is focused on transforming audio or video content such as podcasts, recorded speeches, or other inputs into a variety of types of content.

This content could include suggestions for splicing an existing piece of video or audio into smaller clips, writing blog posts based on the content, creating social media posts, and more.

SwellAI is also a good example of a generative AI that primarily relies on nontext-based inputs, though users do have the ability to provide guidance on outcomes through text-based inputs and a series of menus.

Enterprise-Ready Platforms

The last category of generative AI platforms is what can be termed as ready for the enterprise, or those organizations that have large teams, potentially more extensive data privacy needs (or industry regulations), and that have potentially greater risk if content is released to the public that does not meet a set of standards, which may vary by the company.

OpenAI

In addition to its more consumer-facing versions of ChatGPT, OpenAI offers an enterprise-grade version of the product that protects information entered into it from being used to train its large language models, and even enables users to create their own GPTs that are customizable in their tone and word choice, as well as trainable from existing writing samples.

Writer

A platform that has positioned itself as exclusively tailored for the enterprise company, Writer enables marketers and other teams to create content, govern constraints (such as privacy, legal, regulatory, and others), and analyze the effectiveness of content, all in one platform, and with its own proprietary large language model named Palmyra. This is unique from several other platforms that may put their own unique spin on generative AI output, but still rely on an existing LLM such as OpenAI's GPT-4.

It has several features that enterprise organizations value such as a focus on methods to reduce hallucinations by allowing its generative AI to be trained on company information, while ensuring that any company data fed to its models are not shared with other organizations.

Of course, there are many other platforms out there (after all, that Writerbuddy survey mentioned earlier analyzed over 3,000 AI tools to come up with its list), including ones that generate audio, write software code, create Web page layouts, and more.

EXISTING PLATFORMS WITH ADDED GENERATIVE AI CAPABILITIES

So far, we've focused on brand new AI-based platforms, but there have also been extensive developments of existing platforms that marketers rely on, introducing artificial intelligence features, with a large portion of those being generative AI-focused.

Adobe

Adobe's Creative Cloud includes several software tools used frequently by marketing teams, including Photoshop, Illustrator, InDesign, and more. The company's efforts started with an AI-specific tool called Firefly, which as of September 2023 [ADOBE23] was natively incorporated into its Photoshop, Illustrator, and Adobe Express products.[15]

Adobe's generative AI features allow users to use a text-based prompt to generate images, fill in or remove backgrounds (see Figure 4.3), isolate portions of an image, and much more.

FIGURE 4.3. Image of the Eiffel Tower in Paris where Adobe Photoshop was prompted to "remove background."(Photo courtesy of Greg Kihlström)

The benefits of this approach, rather than using a standalone image generator are many, including a designer or marketer's ability to keep their work within an existing workflow, assuming the creative team utilizes Adobe products for much of its work.

Canva

A popular alternative to Adobe's tools, Canva released its own generative AI capabilities, offering its Magic Design™ tool aimed at simplifying the process that marketers need to use to create unique variations of their designs, as well as designing for the myriad of social media platforms, and other channels they use to reach their customers, such as emails, ads, Web site landing pages, and more.

Salesforce

As one of the leaders in the CRM space, many marketers rely on Salesforce and its ecosystem of products and tools. As of July 2023, the company incorporate generative AI, referred to as Einstein GPT, into several aspects of its products, including the ability for marketers to send more personalized emails, for salespeople to automatically summarize customer interactions, and more [PYMNTS23].[16]

Hubspot

Hubspot is another widespread player in the CRM and marketing automation space with a firm foothold with small and medium-sized businesses, and even some larger organizations. It offers marketing functionality such as email marketing, Web sites and landing pages, social media and advertising capabilities. In addition, it has an entire suite of sales and customer services functionality, with reporting on all of the aforementioned operations.

Similar to how the generative AI capabilities of Photoshop or Canva can rival those of standalone generative AI image-based output tools like DALL-E or Midjourney, Hubspot's Gen AI capabilities have several types of text outputs (and a few related to images), where users can generate emails, landing pages, customer service knowledge bases, and more using text prompts.

Hubspot currently uses OpenAI's large language models for its generative AI functionality.

Of course, there are many more platforms that have incorporated generative AI features, from those geared toward individual marketers for social media content generation and image creation, to enterprises with potentially more complex needs related to search, e-commerce, and more.

HOW GENERATIVE AI CAN BE USED IN MARKETING

While generative AI has the most hype of all of the methods discussed in this section of the book, it is perhaps the least mature in terms of established usage and practices within marketing.

Following are a few ways that generative AI can be used in marketing. Generative AI can quickly analyze large amounts of data to identify patterns and trends in customer behavior, allowing marketers to target their customers more effectively with relevant products and ads. Using effective prompts within a conversational AI interface, marketers can also create personalized content tailored to individual customer preferences and needs, improving the efficiency and accuracy of their campaigns.

Generative AI can also be used to automate tasks such as creating Web site content or design elements efficiently, reducing the time to create content and providing multiple variations that would be time-consuming for humans to create manually.

Additionally, the tools used by generative AI can provide chat responses and mechanisms to provide search results, and even conversational AI tools that have more natural responses to customers.

GENERATIVE AI IN THE ENTERPRISE

Enterprises today are increasingly turning to generative AI to enhance content creation, drive engagement, and sharpen competitiveness. Keep in mind this powerful technology is not without its challenges. Businesses must contend with critical issues such as data security, adherence to legal and regulatory standards, and the imperative to produce on-brand content that resonates with their target audiences.

In the enterprise arena, generative AI must be managed with a nuanced understanding of these pressing concerns:

- **Data Security:** Protecting sensitive information remains paramount for any business, especially when integrating AI systems that process vast data amounts.

- **Legal Compliance:** As AI-generated content becomes commonplace, organizations must ensure their outputs comply with copyright laws, defamation, and other legal constraints.

- **Regulatory Standards:** There are increasing regulatory requirements governing how AI interacts with personal and consumer data, necessitating compliant AI operations.

- **Brand Consistency:** Ensuring that any content created by AI aligns with the company's brand voice and ethos is essential for maintaining brand integrity.

One potential solution for some of these challenges is to use generative AI and retrieval augmented generation (RAG), as its approach can mitigate many of these concerns. RAG uses a method to limit the inputs of generative AI content to only what an enterprise specifies. For instance, this means that if a company wants to train its generative AI only on a specific set of product information, the outputs will not include descriptions of feature sets that are not available or, potentially worse, those that belong to the competition. RAG only looks at what an organization tells it to look at.

This helps in a number of ways:

- **Enhanced Data Security:** By primarily training on a company's existing content repositories, RAG minimizes the risks of exposing sensitive data.

- **Improved Compliance:** RAG systems can be tailored to respect legal and regulatory limits by controlling the corpus on which the AI is trained, ensuring outputs remain within prescribed boundaries.

- **Reduced Misinformation Risks:** The focused training on existing corpora reduces the likelihood of AI "hallucinations," wherein the model generates factually incorrect or misleading content.

- **Consistent Brand Voice:** RAG can deliver outputs that align more closely with a brand's style and message consistency, as it leverages an organization's curated content.

ASSESSMENT

We are still in the early days of generative AI and its usage by marketing teams and departments. But so far, there are definitely some efficiencies to be gained as long as humans review the text and image content created. Because, especially at this relatively early stage in the broad usage of generative AI, it is vital that marketers are not caught off-guard by some of the pitfalls of its usage, such as unauthorized usage of copyrighted material, results that don't make a lot of sense, or results that are based on false or even possibly offensive source material.

Thus, the recommendation at this time is to proceed but with caution. Generative AI is only going to increase in sophistication and usage, so it is not something you want to ignore, but just be cautious about full-scale adoption unless you have a plan to monitor its output.

Additionally, with companies like Adobe, Canva, and Salesforce rapidly adopting AI-based features to legacy tools, it is important that marketers also balance trying out brand new platforms with ensuring that usage of AI will work well with existing workflows. In other words, adopting too many disconnected AI platforms can provide some challenges in determining authorship, ethical usage of data, and other potential issues.

Marketers will need to balance all of these concerns, with guidance from their legal and technology peers where applicable.

NOTES

1   [SARKAR24] Sarkar, Sujan. "AI Industry Analysis: 50 Most Visited AI Tools and Their 24B+ Traffic Behavior." Writerbuddy. Retrieved January 13, 2024 from https://writerbuddy.ai/blog/ai-industry-analysis.

2   [ELIOT23] Eliot, Lance. "Does Exposing andLogging Those Generative AI ChatGPT Erroneous and Hallucinatory Outputs Do Any Good, Asks AI Ethics and AI Law." *Forbes*, para. 7. Retrieved March 4, 2023 from https://www.forbes.com/sites/lanceeliot/2023/01/18/does-exposing-and-logging-those-generative-

ai-chatgpt-erroneous-and-hallucinatory-outputs-do-any-good-asks-ai-ethics-and-ai-law/?sh=439646a26004.

3   [PORTER23] Porter, Jon. "Threads Launches for Nearly Half a Billion More Users in Europe." The Verge. December 14, 2023. Retrieved January 13, 2024 from https://www.theverge.com/2023/12/14/23953986/threads-european-union-launch-eu-meta-twitter-rival.

4   [MCKINSEY23] McKinsey & Company. "What Is Generative AI?" McKinsey & Company. April 2, 2024. Retrieved April 4, 2024 from https://www.mckinsey.com/featured-insights/mckinsey-explainers/what-is-generative-ai.

5   [RUBY23] Ruby, Daniel. "ChatGPT Statistics for 2023: Comprehensive Facts and Data." DemandSage. February 8, 2023. Retrieved March 4, 2023 from https://www.demandsage.com/chatgpt-statistics/.

6   [TONG23] Tong, Anna. "Exclusive: ChatGPT Traffic Slips Again for Third Month in a Row." Reuters. September 7, 2023. Retrieved January 13, 2024 from https://www.reuters.com/technology/chatgpt-traffic-slips-again-third-month-row-2023-09-07/.

7   [CAPOOT23] Capoot, Ashley. "Microsoft Announces New Multibillion-Dollar Investment in ChatGPT-Maker Open AI." CNBC. January 23, 2023. Retrieved March 4, 2023 from `https://www.cnbc.com/2023/01/23/microsoft-announces-multibillion-dollar-investment-in-chatgpt-maker-openai.html.

8   [ALBA23] Alba, Davey, and Julia Love. "Google Releases ChatGPT Rival AI 'Bard' to Early Testers." *Los Angeles Times*. February 6, 2023. Retrieved January 13, 2024 from https://www.latimes.com/business/story/2023-02-06/google-chatgpt-rival-ai-bard-early-testers.

9   [PIERCE24] Pierce, David. "Google's AI Now Goes by a New Name: Gemini." The Verge. February 8, 2024. Retrieved April 4, 2024 from https://www.theverge.com/2024/2/8/24065553/google-gemini-ios-android-app-duet-bard.

10 [PATRIZIO24] Patrizio, Andy. "Definition: Google Bard." TechTarget. Retrieved January 13, 2024 from https://www.techtarget.com/searchenterpriseai/definition/Google-Bard.

11 [VICTOR23] Victor, Jon, and Aaron Holmes. "OpenAI Is Making Headlines. It's Also Seeding Talent Across Silicon Valley." The Information. Februrary 1, 2023. Retrieved April 4, 2024 from https://www.theinformation.com/articles/openai-is-making-headlines-its-also-seeding-talent-across-silicon-valley.

12 [VINCENT23] Vincent, James "AI Art Tools Stable Diffusion and Midjourney Targeted with Copyright Lawsuit." The Verge. January 16, 2023. Retrieved

April 4, 2024 from https://www.theverge.com/2023/1/16/23557098/generative-ai-art-copyright-legal-lawsuit-stable-diffusion-midjourney-deviantart.

13 [BROOKS24] Brooks, Tim et. al. "Video Generation Models as World Simulators." OpenAI.com Retrieved February 24, 2024 from https://openai.com/research/video-generation-models-as-world-simulators

14 [JASPER23] Jasper. Home page. Retrieved February 11, 2023 from https://www.jasper.ai/.

15 [ADOBE23] Adobe. "Adobe Announces All New AI-Powered Creative Cloud Release." Adobe Web site. September 13, 2023. Retrieved January 13, 2024 from https://news.adobe.com/news/news-details/2023/Adobe-Announces-All-New-AI-Powered-Creative-Cloud-Release-default.aspx/default.aspx.

16 [PYMNTS23] PYMNTS. "Salesforce Introduces Generative AI Tools for Sales and Service." PYMNTS. July 19, 2023. Retrieved January 13, 2024 from https://www.pymnts.com/artificial-intelligence-2/2023/salesforce-introduces-generative-ai-tools-for-sales-and-service/.

CHAPTER 5

PERSONALIZED CUSTOMER EXPERIENCE

While there are many ways that artificial intelligence is shaping the way companies interact with their customers, a particularly effective one is by creating a more personalized customer experiences and creating efficiencies in the ability to reach customers on their platform(s) of choice. With AI, businesses can gain valuable insights into customer data and develop tailored strategies that are better targeted toward each individual customer's needs.

SOME EXAMPLES OF AI-AUGMENTED CUSTOMER EXPERIENCES

The following sections explore a few of these customer experiences that are improved by the use of artificial intelligence tools and methods.

Personalized Content, Offers, and Experiences

AI-driven models can be used to create personalized content and offer for customers based on their demographics, psychographics, purchase history, and a myriad of personal preferences or past behaviors. By analyzing customer actions plus past behaviors in real-time, AI models can generate highly relevant content tailored to each customer's interests and propensity to purchase.

Furthermore, businesses can also use predictive analytics to anticipate customer behavior and proactively intervene with messages or promotions before the decision to buy or abandon is made.

Overall, AI-driven solutions provide businesses with powerful tools to build stronger customer relationships by creating engaging, tailored experiences that drive sales. This helps engage customers while providing them with an enhanced user experience. It also helps businesses maximize customer lifetime value and reduce the likelihood that customers will abandon carts, cancel subscriptions, or choose a competitor instead.

Conversational AI

Conversational AI is yet another way that artificial intelligence technologies can be used to create a more engaging and personalized customer experience. A few levels of complexity are available in this and its broader category of conversational marketing. The simplest form is what is often referred to as a "chatbot," providing a simplified multiple-choice menu of options for users to select and proceed through a number of steps. A more complex form is what is referred to as conversational AI, which allows customers to freely type (rather than choose from a preset selection of options) what they need in the form of questions, phrases, or paragraphs. Most people have likely seen this and even interacted with one at multiple points, as illustrated in Figure 5.1.

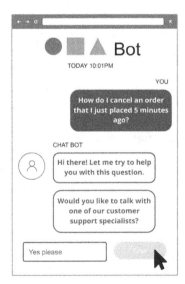

FIGURE 5.1. An example of a chatbot or conversational AI interface.

With this more intelligent chat technology (which will be referred to as "conversational AI" throughout the remainder of the book), businesses can conversationally interact with customers, allowing them to ask and answer questions in natural language. This allows customers to obtain the information they need quickly and easily while also providing companies with valuable insights into their customer's needs and preferences, including the words and methods they use to describe their problems or challenges and the potential solutions.

Additionally, conversational AI can be used to deliver personalized content based on customer data such as demographics, purchase history, and personal preferences when connected to other internal systems. This helps ensure customers are presented with the most relevant messages based on their current context, leading to an improved user experience. By utilizing conversational AI, companies can create more meaningful relationships with their customers by delivering personalized content tailored to their individual needs and interests.

Journey Orchestration

Customer journey orchestration (CJO) is a multichannel approach to delivering personalized customer experiences, which works by guiding customers through the buyer's journey (and beyond), showing the most relevant content, offers, and even campaigns that maximize the likelihood of resulting in a conversion. Customer Journey Orchestration platforms allow organizations to map each step or potential step in a customer's lifecycle, as illustrated in Figure 5.2, and associate a set of criteria that either trigger a response, or indicate that a step has been completed to move that customer to the next step in their journey.

By leveraging AI tools, including machine learning models, customer journey orchestration can analyze customer data, such as demographics, purchasing patterns, and preferences, in order to anticipate customer behavior and intervene with relevant messages before a purchase or abandonment decision is made, or send messages on the channel or using the method that the customer prefers or is most likely to respond through. For instance, a customer may prefer getting SMS messages over email or be a heavy user of the brand's mobile app; thus, a push notification will be most effective in reaching them. This allows businesses to customize the content they deliver so that it is tailored to each individual's current context.

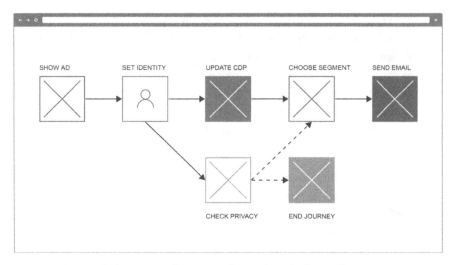

FIGURE 5.2. A customer journey orchestration platform allows users to map journeys and the steps that customers can take, as well as their interactions.

CJO also helps companies track customer engagements across multiple channels and devices to gain deeper insights into customers' preferences, needs, and interests, providing a unified view of the customer—often with the help of a customer data platform (CDP), which enables the collection and unification of data points across first, second, and third parties. This allows businesses to create a unified experience for customers regardless of their channel or device. Overall, utilizing AI-driven tools such as customer journey orchestration helps businesses build stronger relationships with their customers by delivering them engaging content tailored to their individual needs and interests.

The sheer amount of acquisitions in the CJO space means that there is and will be a lot of attention on it in the months and years ahead. Kitewheel was purchased by CSG in mid-2021 and renamed XPonent [CSG21],[1] Thunderhead was recently acquired by Medallia in early 2022 [RODGERS22],[2] and Pointillist was acquired by Genesys in 2021 [SMITH21],[3] to name three of the more prominent names in the space.

Next Best Action

Similar in some ways to customer journey orchestration, next best action (NBA) is a strategy that uses AI to provide customers with relevant, personalized recommendations based on their current context to maximize engagement and optimize customer experiences. It diverges from CJO in that next best action is often less prescriptive in its approach to what exactly that next best or desired action should be. An orchestrated journey is often (though not always) created from the perspective of what the brand would like a relevant customer to do next, while NBA can be thought of as a little more freeform in its approach, allowing a customer or prospect's next best action to be related to a completely different product or service than their initial starting point or recommended action.

While this may sound a little too unbounded for many marketers, there can be guardrails in place to ensure business objectives are still factored into recommendations. Propensity to buy, balanced with business "levers," can then provide next best action or offer to a customer that meets both the customer's needs and the needs of the business.

HOW GREATER PERSONALIZATION IS CHANGING MARKETING

There are several ways that greater personalization, driven by AI-based tools, is changing the way the marketers are performing their jobs, as well as creating strategies for the future. Let's explore a few of these.

Marketing Approach

Personalized customer experiences are changing the way marketers work by enabling deeper and more intelligent segmentation and more relevant offers, content, and experiences that need to be designed but have the potential to be more compelling and thus perform better than one-size-fits-all approaches.

Manually creating multiple variations of content is more work than creating a single version or even one or two for an A/B test. Thus, generative AI holds a lot of promise to be used in conjunction with approaches like CJO and next best action because there can be infinite variations of journeys, content, offers, and experiences that the two approaches work hand-in-virtual hand to create.

The other big change is a shift away from running single campaigns at a time into running many parallel campaigns and using AI, CJO, next best action, and customers IRL (in real life), self-selecting the most relevant campaign to them. After all, an approach such as next best action requires that many different options could potentially be that next best action rather than a single choice or . . . nothing.

Gone are the days that spawned Henry Ford's famous quote that customers could have a Ford Model T in any color—as long as it was black. Today's customers want a custom-colored car, made to order with the features that specifically match their needs.

The Customer Perspective

The use of AI to personalize customer experiences has profoundly affected customers in many ways. First, it helps customers find and access relevant content faster than ever before. By leveraging AI-driven technologies such as machine learning models, companies can analyze customer data to anticipate their needs and present them with the most relevant content according to their current context. This helps customers find the products or services they seek more quickly and easily.

In addition, using AI to personalize the customer experience also makes it easier for customers to stay informed about products and services that may interest them. By monitoring customer engagements across multiple channels and devices, companies can gain deeper insights into what customers want and target them with offers or messages based on their particular interests. This helps ensure that customers are presented with content tailored specifically for them, thus enhancing the overall customer experience.

There are conflicting statistics about consumers' preferences toward personalization. For instance, a recent Pantheon study [SCHULTZ23] found that 64% of consumers prefer generic messages to personalized content. Yet, in that same report, 73% of customers are willing to share information with the expectation that they will receive personalized experiences.[4] And these numbers conflict with many findings that show that personalization increases shopping, purchases, and repeat purchases.

That said, a takeaway that supports both sides of the coin, so to speak, is that consumers only want to share information with brands that they trust, and when they share it, they expect the personalization to be meaningful.

ASSESSMENT

If a business is not personalizing customer experiences to some degree, they are already behind the competition. Even basic personalization is table stakes these days, and many customers want more from their brands. After all, customers provide a lot of information to the companies they are loyal to, and in return, they expect that those brands provide a valuable and relevant experience in return.

It is past time for businesses to be considering customer journey orchestration and next best action capabilities for marketing, however they should be warned that these will require some work if customer data and marketing technology infrastructure lacks integration across channels and touchpoints. That said, there's no time like the present to get started because the competition is doing the same, if not a couple of steps ahead by this point.

NOTES

1   [CSG21] CSG. "CSG Supercharges Customer Engagement Solutions with Acquisition of Kitewheel." CSG. July 13, 2021. Retrieved March 4, 2023 from https://ir.csgi.com/investors/press-releases/press-release-details/2021/CSG-Supercharges-Customer-Engagement-Solutions-with-Acquisition-of-Kitewheel/.

2   [RODGERS22] Rodgers, Gabrielle."Medallia to Acquire Journey Orchestration Provider Thunderhead." CMSWire. January 26, 2022. Retrieved March 4, 2023 from https://www.cmswire.com/customer-experience/medallia-to-acquire-journey-orchestration-provider-thunderhead/.

3   [SMITH21] Smith, William. "Genesys Completes Acquisition of Pointillist and Exceed.ai." CX Today. December 3, 2021. Retrieved March 4, 2023 from https://www.cxtoday.com/contact-centre/genesys-completes-acquisition-of-pointillist-and-exceed-ai/.

4   [SCHULTZ23] Schultz, Ray. "Consumers Prefer Generic Messages to Personalized Ones, Study Finds." MediaPost. January 30, 2023. Retrieved March 4, 2023 from https://www.mediapost.com/publications/article/382043/consumers-prefer-generic-messages-to-personalized.html.

CHAPTER 6

TEAM AND WORKFLOW AUGMENTATION

The next area we're going to talk about is hardly a new one, and such, it can sometimes be overlooked in the conversation about AI utilization for marketers. We talked about robotic process automation, or RPA, in the previous section of the book because it is an area where AI is already being heavily used in business, although perhaps it is less glamorous than other areas, such as generative AI. Even so, there are compelling statistics about how RPA can augment teams' capabilities and their ability to produce quality work.

And while there is some concern about AI or machines replacing people's roles at work, 60% of executives surveyed in a recent Forrester report [KIRKWOOD19] seem to agree that RPA enables people to focus on more strategic work, and nearly the same amount of those same executives (57%) claim RPA increases employee engagement while reducing manual errors.[1]

The struggle, as they say, is real, and the move to hybrid and remote work has, in some ways, exacerbated certain issues with repetitive and time-consuming tasks that RPA and workflow automation do better than humans. After all, in a fully remote, or even hybrid work situation, the idea of turning to ask a fellow employee at the next desk over to help with something is gone, and even with collaboration tools like Zoom, Teams, Slack, and others, there has been a need to adjust how work gets done, and how quick interactions occur in the work environment.

So, what is to be done about it? There are a number of ways to solve these challenges, and several are explored in the following sections.

SOME EXAMPLES OF PROCESS AUTOMATION IN MARKETING

Process automation is an increasingly popular tool in marketing, allowing marketers to automate and streamline their tasks and make them more efficient. Following are three examples of how marketers and their teams can use process and workflow automation.

Automated Workflows

This type of process automation helps to streamline mundane tasks such as data entry, email creation and scheduling, campaign management, lead qualification and tracking, and more. By automating these types of tasks, marketers can save time and focus on developing creative campaigns that will really drive engagement.

In the marketing and communications world, an example is the product PRophet, founded by a PR firm executive, Aaron Kwitken. PRophet streamlines the media pitching process, which, when done manually, can take countless hours of research, emails, phone calls, and other laborious tasks. By contrast, the platform uses AI to analyze a pitch and suggests the best journalists to reach out to based on a number of proprietary factors using natural language processing and machine learning to provide the best possible candidates.

Personalization

Although discussed in the previous chapter from a customer perspective, but it is helpful to look at personalization from a marketer and employee perspective as well, as it can help marketing teams with customer segmentation and personalization. By leveraging machine learning algorithms, marketers can analyze customer data such as demographics, purchasing patterns, and preferences to more accurately target customer segments with personalized messaging.

While this certainly helps customers to have a better experience through personalization, it also enables marketers to be more effective in their work by automating complex steps and enabling them to spend more time on the strategy and approach and less time on marketing execution. Plus, mass personalization for millions of customers simply isn't something that even a large marketing team can do without the help of automation.

Reporting and Analytics

Finally, process automation allows marketers to track customer engagements across multiple channels and gain insights into what content resonates most with each customer by filtering, audience segments, or other criteria. This helps ensure that customers are being presented with content that is relevant and tailored specifically for them, thus enhancing the overall customer experience.

Overall, process automation provides a great way for marketers to save time and resources while still delivering engaging experiences to their customers.

A 2020 survey by Pegasystems [PEGA20], a big player in the RPA space, confirmed that 63% of global executives say RPA goes hand-in-hand with digital transformation initiatives.[2]

HOW IT IS CHANGING MARKETING

Following are a few ways that AI-based workflow automation and team augmentation are changing how marketing is done.

Strategic Marketing Approach

Remember, when AI is used most effectively, it augments what humans do best: being more creative, innovative, and strategic rather than focused on repetitive tasks. Thus, marketers can create more effective strategies and campaigns when they are able to take advantage of AI automation technology.

Example marketing workflow automation

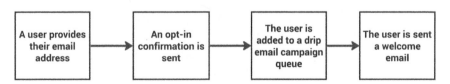

FIGURE 6.1. A simple marketing automation workflow.

A simple example of automation, as shown in Figure 6.1, is something like the following:

1. A user provides their email address, submitting it through a Web form on a landing page.

2. When the form is submitted, it automatically triggers an opt-in confirmation email to be sent.

3. Once the user opts in, they are added to an email list that is scheduled to receive a drip email campaign.

4. This adds the user to a queue to receive a welcome email, likely the first email in a series of messages in a drip campaign.

By leveraging automation, marketers can focus more time on planning and executing tailored marketing initiatives instead of wasting man-hours on mundane tasks. Marketers can generate better outcomes with less effort by allowing AI-driven systems to automate large portions of the workload.

AI automation also improves accuracy in things like data analysis, segmentation, and marketing intelligence gathering. With robust insights generated by AI algorithms, marketers can make better decisions about their marketing strategies that will yield better results. Additionally, this type of automation enables marketers to work smarter and faster to quickly adjust course if needed or capitalize on any sudden opportunities that arise in the market.

Going back to our example in Figure 6.1, if we add some more intelligent AI-based automation, we might detect that the user is based in Spain, thus sending them an opt-in email that incorporates consumer data privacy language specific to the European Union's GDPR regulations.

Additionally, if the user is an existing customer that filled out a welcome form by accident, our AI-based system should be smart enough to add them to a different marketing queue altogether, as a long-standing customer will likely not need to be guided through the welcome process. Instead, we might add them to another list and campaign for existing customers.

Overall, leveraging AI for automated tasks provides a framework for marketers to improve their strategies and campaigns over time with greater efficiency and effectiveness.

Streamlining Workflows

The second big way AI is used for team and workflow automation in changing marketing is by enabling complex or inconsistent workstreams to become more managed and consistent. Streamlining workflow processes for marketing teams can have a number of benefits, from increased productivity to better creative output. By decluttering the marketing process and keeping team members focused on their specific tasks, marketers can work faster and more efficiently. Streamlining also encourages collaboration between departments, allowing for better communication and a greater sense of unification among the marketing team.

Streamlined workflows also allow marketers to access real-time data that helps them make informed decisions quickly and accurately. With AI-based systems providing reliable data on user interaction with products or services, marketers can identify trends faster and respond accordingly. Additionally, streamlining can help marketers identify areas where further automation may be helpful in reducing overhead costs associated with manual processes. Overall, streamlining workflows is an effective way to improve marketing teams' performance and create better results.

Automating Repetitive Tasks

Like streamlining workflows, automating repetitive tasks can be a powerful tool to help marketers do better work. By offloading mundane tasks such as content creation, data collection, and analytics reporting, marketers can focus on higher-level tasks requiring more creativity and strategic thinking. Automation also enables marketers to quickly access customer data and make changes in real-time, allowing them to adjust their strategies continuously for maximum impact.

Using AI for automating repetitive tasks provides additional insights into customers' behaviors, preferences, and interests. With AI-based systems continuously collecting data from customers' interactions with products or services, marketers have access to accurate metrics than can be used to develop strategies that are tailored to individual customers. This level of customization is helping brands deliver personalized experiences that lead to increased engagement and conversion rates.

Improving the Customer Experience

This section explores workflow automation and its benefit to customers. Streamlining internal processes is not only good for internal teams—it's a great way to improve the customer experience. By focusing on efficiency and optimizing workflow, companies can ensure that customer inquiries are answered quickly and accurately, leading to higher satisfaction with the service they receive. Streamlining can also help eliminate inefficiencies caused by manual processes and enable customers to self-serve tasks that traditionally took more time or resources.

Streamlining internal workflows also allows for improved communication between teams. By ensuring all departments have access to customer data, marketers can better tailor campaigns or services to individual needs and provide personalized experiences that result in better engagement and loyalty. Moreover, streamlining helps reduce errors as automated systems can be set up to quickly flag any discrepancies in customer data so that they may be rectified promptly.

When done correctly, streamlining internal workflows can significantly improve the overall customer experience by providing fast response times, tailored solutions, and lower error rates. Companies can deliver high-quality service while staying cost-effective and productive. This results in higher customer satisfaction, which is essential for businesses today looking to create loyal customers out of every interaction.

ASSESSMENT

Automation is often about cost savings and productivity at the end of the day, so any evaluation of AI-based tools for automation should take both of these into account. After all, if automating your workflow isn't making your teams more efficient, why bother implementing them in the first place?

Even though AI-based automation has been around for a long time (at least comparatively), it also has a lot of potentials to continue to grow and evolve. It also has the potential to continue focusing human teams on what they do best, while the machines can take care of the rest.

NOTES

1 [KIRKWOOD19] Kirkwood, Guy. "The Impact of RPA on Employee Engagement, a Forrester Consulting Thought Leadership Paper." UIPath. March 15, 2019. Retrieved March 4, 2023 from https://www.uipath.com/resources/automation-analyst-reports/forrester-employee-experience-rpa.

2 [PEGA20] Pega. "RPA and Digital Transformation: Why Immediate Benefits Do Not Translate Into a Long-Term Solution." Pega White Paper. Retrieved March 4, 2023 from https://www.pega.com/system/files/resources/2020-01/rpa-and-digital-transformation-report.pdf.

CHAPTER 7

DATA ANALYSIS, MEASUREMENT, AND OPTIMIZATION

This chapter explores how artificial intelligence (AI) and machine learning can be used to improve marketing efforts through analytics and tracking, with the goal of continuously improving them.

AI and machine learning have a lot to offer marketers who want to get the most out of their data and take their campaigns further through predictive, personalized, and continuous learning approaches. By leveraging AI technology to understand customer needs and patterns better, marketers can optimize their strategies for greater returns on investment in time and money. Furthermore, with enhanced segmentation capabilities, marketers can create tailored campaigns for different customer profiles to achieve higher engagement levels. Finally, with intelligent budget optimization algorithms, companies can maximize ROI by adjusting spending according to predictive outcomes.

SOME EXAMPLES OF AI USED IN DATA ANALYSIS, MEASUREMENT, AND OPTIMIZATION

Imagine a marketer for a large retail company who has access to a dataset generated by AI that predicts customer segmentation based on various factors such as demographics, purchase history, browsing behavior, and so on. This dataset can be used to identify high-value customers, potential churners, and other customer segments that require specific marketing strategies.

Some potential applications of this dataset could be one (or more) of the following:

- **Personalized Marketing Messages:** Use the dataset to create personalized marketing messages for each customer segment based on their preferences, interests, and purchase history.

- **Customer Retention Strategies:** Identify potential churners and develop targeted retention strategies to keep them engaged and purchasing from your brand.

- **Product Recommendations:** Use the dataset to suggest relevant products to customers based on their purchase history, browsing behavior, and preferences.

- **Audience Targeting:** Use the dataset to create lookalike audiences for social media advertising, search marketing, and other digital marketing channels.

- **Marketing Attribution Modeling:** Use the dataset to develop a more accurate attribution model that takes into account the impact of various touchpoints on customer purchases and loyalty.

The following explores a few more examples of how we can augment measurement and optimization in our marketing using artificial intelligence and related tools and methods.

Predictive Analytics

Predictive analytics is a powerful tool for marketers that helps to gain insights into customer behavior and identify opportunities for improved strategic decisions, whether automated or manually. It leverages data mining, statistical modeling, and machine learning algorithms to generate predictions based on past customer interactions with a brand and potential future actions.

Predictive analytics can be used to understand better what customers want or need, tailor campaigns and promotions more effectively, assess the success rate of various strategies, segment customer data for more targeted messaging, and identify budget optimization tactics to maximize ROI. Here are three unique uses of predictive analytics in marketing:

1. The first use is in segmenting customer data. Predictive analytics can help marketers identify which customer data segments can be targeted with more successful campaigns, leading to higher engagement and sales. By analyzing past customer behavior, marketers gain insights into potential future behaviors that could be used to create better-segmented promotions or services geared toward particular audiences.

2. Another use of predictive analytics is in assessing the success rate of various strategies. By leveraging machine learning models, marketers can look at how different strategies have affected campaign results and make predictions about how they may perform under certain conditions in the future. In this way, marketers can adjust their tactics quickly and accurately to optimize their performance over time.

3. Finally, predictive analytics also helps with budget optimization by calculating the money necessary for investment into each customer segment. With precise projections of long-term ROI, companies can structure budgets accordingly for maximum efficiency and cost savings without sacrificing quality or performance objectives.

Overall, predictive analytics provides valuable insights into how customers interact with brands and empowers marketing teams with a comprehensive understanding of customer behavior so they can take better-informed actions when it comes to creating campaigns or launching new products.

Audience Segment Optimization

Marketers can use AI-based solutions to optimize audience segments for more successful customer experiences. By analyzing customer profiles, demographic data, purchase patterns, and other important factors, AI models can segment customers into targeted groups more likely to respond to marketing messages. Marketers may start with a more basic set of segments that are then refined through analysis by AI. This optimized segmentation reduces wasted time and resources on ineffective campaigns and leads to better results overall.

Furthermore, AI-driven segmentation algorithms can use predictive analytics to identify either new behaviors that would dictate creating a new type of segment or even when a particular customer might be more identifiable with a different segment than the one they currently belong to. Such algorithms can also be used to identify previously untapped opportunities across different customer segments, allowing companies to explore new markets or introduce new offerings based on changing consumer preferences. Thus, artificial intelligence can help marketers gain invaluable insights to make informed decisions when crafting effective audience segments.

Propensity

Artificial intelligence can be used to calculate propensity, or the likelihood of customer conversion, regardless of the type of conversion needed. AI algorithms analyze various data points, such as the customer's past behavior, demographics, psychographics, and other factors, to accurately predict whether a customer is likely to convert their preferred communication channel and their likelihood to drop out of the funnel altogether. This enables marketers to target potential customers with high levels of accuracy, allowing them to focus their resources on those with the highest likelihood of converting.

By leveraging predictive analytics, AI models can uncover hidden correlations between different customer segments and better understand their preferences for effective marketing campaigns. Additionally, AI models can also detect subtle changes in customer behavior over time, which could indicate an increased or decreased propensity for conversion. Then, by combining numerous data sources from disparate systems within an organization (both structured and unstructured), these AI models enable marketers to gain insights that would otherwise be impossible to achieve manually. This helps marketers make better decisions when calculating budgets and allocating resources more efficiently.

Using resources more efficiently might consist of spending more advertising dollars where customers are likely to convert and deprioritizing efforts to convert unlikely buyers. Additionally, depending on the customer lifetime value model, it may calculate that it is worthwhile to offer some customers steep discounts or loss-leading offers to get them in the door and grow their value over time. Likewise, these models may be able to distinguish between those likely to be lifetime customers versus those who are one-time buyers and then make decisions over what type of offers and discounts to provide based on the potential lifetime value.

HOW AI IS CHANGING MARKETING

Artificial intelligence (AI) is transforming how marketers think about analytics and optimization through the methods discussed earlier in this chapter. It enables marketers to develop smarter strategies that better target the right customers at the right time, with the right message, and on the right channel.

In addition, there are several other benefits for marketers in using AI-based tools for data analysis, measurement, and optimization, including:

- **Increased Efficiency:** By using AI-generated datasets, marketers can automate many tasks such as segmentation, message personalization, and audience targeting, freeing up more time for strategic planning and creative work.

- **Improved Accuracy:** AI-generated datasets can provide more accurate predictions and recommendations based on large amounts of data, leading to better marketing outcomes and higher ROI.

- **Enhanced Customer Experience:** By using personalization, recommendation engines, and lookalike audiences powered by AI-generated datasets, marketers can deliver a more tailored and engaging customer experience that drives loyalty and advocacy.

- **Better Decision Making:** With access to more accurate and comprehensive data, marketers can make better decisions about which marketing strategies to pursue, how to allocate budget, and when to adjust course based on performance metrics.

Overall, the use of AI-generated datasets in marketing can lead to a more efficient, effective, and customer-centric approach to marketing that drives better business outcomes and builds brand loyalty over time.

MIXING AI-BASED DATA ANALYSIS WITH GENERATIVE AI

Another approach that can yield beneficial results is to mix some of the AI methods to capitalize on areas of overlap where each can help each other out leverage results not possible with a single method alone. One example of this is mixing a text-based chat interface to a marketing analysis and reporting tool.

For instance, a marketer would be presented with a chat interface where they could type a question such as, "have we had more event registrations for webinars this month versus last month?"

The chat interface would interpret that prompt and work with a data analysis and reporting tool to answer that question. This could be in the form of a text-based output (e.g. "Yes, there was a 10% increase in webinar registrations for this month from last month") or even a chart of graphics depicting the increase.

This enables non data scientists and those for which poring through rows of data or using analytics platforms is not their responsibility to get answers to crucial questions that help them perform their jobs much easier.

ASSESSMENT

There is a shift away from analytics and data analysis being done primarily (or solely) after an event occurs to something occurring as events unfold. While this is not a completely new phenomenon—predictive and real-time analytics have been around for years—its increased adoption and the growing number of tools that utilize it are hitting a new peak.

Building on existing experimentation and multivariate testing tools, predictive and real-time analytics, combined with more sophisticated audience segmentation, provides marketers with new and more dynamic ways of reaching customers where they are with what they need, on the channels, and with the offers that are most likely to convert.

This shift for marketers means that predictive and real-time analytics are now more accessible, and analytics as a practice does not have to be primarily after the fact. Additionally, by incorporating generative AI, chat-style interfaces with analytics and reporting tools, any marketer can use natural language questions to query campaign results to get quick and accurate answers to their questions.

With the ability to take predictive and real-time data, analyze it utilizing AI and machine learning models, and react in near-real-time to customer needs, marketers can be more responsive than ever before.

PRACTICAL EXAMPLES

M oving forward, the text will transition from the more foundational AI knowledge to applying generative AI in the marketing field with some practical examples of prompt-based inputs that are designed to achieve optimal results. Here, the bridge is gapped between theoretical knowledge and actionable application, focusing on how generative AI prompts can assist marketers in the creation of images, text, and the analysis of marketing data.

By the end of Part III, readers will not only have a solid grasp of how to implement generative AI in various marketing contexts but hopefully also feel inspired to experiment and innovate within your own campaigns. This is geared toward embracing the evolving landscape of marketing, where AI becomes a critical tool in one's arsenal for driving creativity, engagement, and ultimately, success in a digital-first world.

IMPROVING PROMPT WRITING

While previous chapters have explored several types of artificial intelligence-based tools, the popularity of generative AI is clear, and marketers are one of its key adopters.

Gen AI offers great potential in terms of its outputs, but it still needs its human counterparts to provide good inputs in order to get marketers what they need to achieve their goals. This means that marketers need to be more skilled at writing *prompts* or the text-based instructions that generative AI tools use to write blog posts on the best hotels to visit in Tokyo during the summer, generate images or Stockholm's city center during snowfall, or create a video of an alien spaceship flying over the Buenos Aires skyline.

The following sections explore what it means to write a good prompt, as well as some practices to avoid, to get higher quality and more efficient results.

BE SPECIFIC AND CLEAR

The more specific and clear a prompt is, the more specific and relevant the generated content will be. Users should avoid vague or open-ended prompts that may confuse the AI model.

Here's an example of a specific and clear prompt for generative AI:

```
Write a short story about a group of friends who go
on a camping trip and discover a mysterious object in
```

the woods that changes their lives forever. The story should be written in a humorous and lighthearted tone, with vivid descriptions of the natural setting and the characters' interactions. Include elements of adventure, surprise, and self-discovery, and make sure the story is appropriate for all ages.

This prompt is specific and clear because it:

- **Provides a clear scenario:** The prompt gives a specific situation (a group of friends on a camping trip) and a clear goal (discovering a mysterious object).

- **Uses descriptive language:** The prompt includes vivid descriptions of the natural setting and the characters' interactions, which helps the AI understand the desired tone and style.

- **Includes specific elements:** The prompt includes specific elements such as adventure, surprise, and self-discovery, which helps guide the AI in producing content that is relevant and engaging.

- **Specifies the target audience:** The prompt is appropriate for all ages, which helps ensure that the generated content is suitable for a wide range of readers.

- **Uses a consistent tone and style:** The prompt uses a humorous and lighthearted tone, which helps establish a clear and recognizable voice for the generated content.

USE SIMPLE LANGUAGE

AI models work best with simple, straightforward language. Avoid using complex sentences, jargon, or technical terms that may be difficult for the model to understand.

Here are two examples of prompts:

Simple Language Prompt

"Write a story about a group of friends who go on a camping trip and discover a mysterious object in the woods. The story should be fun and exciting, with vivid descriptions of the natural setting and the characters' interactions."

Complex, Jargony Prompt

"Generate a narrative that incorporates themes of adventure, discovery, and self-actualization, set against a backdrop of a pristine wilderness landscape. The story should be infused with a sense of wonder and awe and feature a diverse cast of characters who must navigate a series of challenges and obstacles to achieve their goals."

The simple language prompt is preferred because it:

- **Uses clear and concise language:** The prompt is easy to understand and free of ambiguity. For instance, it states that the story should be about a "group of friends" while the complex prompt simply talks about abstract concepts and a "diverse cast of characters" that should be incorporated.

- **Avoids jargon:** The prompt does not use technical terms or specialized language that may be difficult for the AI to interpret.

- **Provides a clear scenario:** The prompt gives a specific situation (a group of friends on a camping trip) and a clear goal (discovering a mysterious object).

- **Specifies the target audience:** The prompt is appropriate for all ages, which helps ensure that the generated content is suitable for a wide range of readers.

The complex jargon prompt may be difficult for the AI to understand and interpret because:

- **It uses technical terms:** The prompt includes specialized language such as "adventure," "discovery," and "self-actualization" that may be unfamiliar to the AI.

- **It is vague:** The prompt does not provide a clear scenario or goal, leaving the AI with too much room for interpretation.

- **It uses overly complex language:** The prompt includes words and phrases that are unlikely to be found in everyday language, such as "infused with a sense of wonder and awe."

PROVIDE CONTEXT

Context is essential when writing prompts for generative AI because it helps the AI understand the purpose and goals of the content it generates. This can include information about the target audience, tone, style, and any relevant keywords or themes. Without proper context, the AI may produce content that is irrelevant, inappropriate, or misunderstood.

Here's an example of how marketers can provide context when writing prompts for generative AI:

```
Write a social media post promoting our new line of
eco-friendly cleaning products. The post should be
engaging, informative, and highlight the benefits of
using our products. Consider including a catchy headline,
vivid imagery, and a clear call to action.
```

This example has a number of elements of context that will be helpful to generative AI, and you can see the results of providing this prompt to ChatGPT in Figure 8.1. The prompt does the following well:

- **Defines the target audience:** In this example, the target audience is individuals who prioritize eco-friendliness and sustainability when purchasing cleaning products. Providing context helps the AI understand the demographics and psychographics of the intended audience.

- **Specifies the desired tone and style:** The desired tone and style should be consistent with the brand's overall messaging and personality. In this example, the tone could be playful and engaging, with a focus on the benefits of using eco-friendly cleaning products.

- **Provides contextual information:** To help the AI understand the content it generates, provide contextual information such as the product line's unique selling points, key features, and competitive differentiators. This information can be used to create a cohesive and consistent message across all generated content.

- **Uses concrete language:** Instead of using vague terms like "eco-friendly," use concrete language that describes the specific benefits of the products. For example, "our new line of cleaning products is made with plant-based ingredients, biodegradable materials, and minimal packaging to reduce waste."

- **Includes clear objectives:** Clear objectives help guide the AI in producing content that aligns with the desired tone and style. In this example, the objective could be "generate a social media post that increases brand awareness and drives sales of our new line of eco-friendly cleaning products."

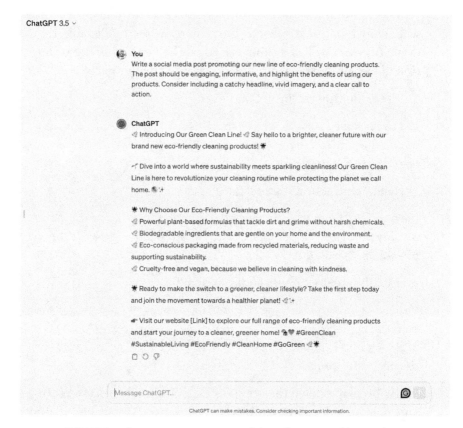

FIGURE 8.1. A prompt to create a social media post and its results as generated by ChatGPT.

BREAK DOWN COMPLEX TASKS

If you have a complex task, break it down into smaller, more manageable parts. This will help the AI model to focus on one aspect at a time and generate higher quality content.

For instance, you might have the following as a task you'd like to send as a single prompt:

Generate a comprehensive marketing plan for a new product launch, including identifying the target audience, crafting a brand message, and creating a multimedia campaign.

If you are able to break it down into smaller pieces, it is likely you will achieve better results, as the generative AI tool is able to focus on doing one part well at a time. Based on the need from the prompt mentioned earlier, here it is broken down into smaller parts:

First, identify the target audience:

Write a description of the ideal customer for our new product, including demographics, psychographics, and purchasing habits.

Then, craft a brand message:

Develop a unique and compelling tagline, as well as a set of key messaging points that capture the essence of our brand and product.

Finally, create a multimedia campaign:

Design a series of social media posts, videos, and email marketing campaigns that showcase our product's features and benefits, and create a sense of urgency and excitement around the launch.

By breaking down the complex task into smaller parts, more specific and manageable prompts for the generative AI can be created. Each prompt focuses on one specific aspect of the marketing plan, making it easier for the AI to generate high-quality content that is relevant and engaging. Additionally, by breaking down the task into smaller parts, it is possible to reduce the risk of overwhelming the AI with too much information or too many competing priorities.

USE POSITIVE LANGUAGE

Frame your prompts in positive terms, focusing on what you want the AI model to generate rather than what you don't want. For example, instead of "don't use clichés," you can use a prompt that says, "generate unique and compelling content."

Using too many negative prompts or language is a sure way to get inconsistent results from your prompts. Remember, artificial intelligence is smart (and getting smarter), but can still get tripped up with commands and words that it can find confusing or conflicting.

PROVIDE SPECIFIC EXAMPLES

If possible, users should provide examples of the type of content they want the AI model to generate. This can help to clarify intent and guide the model toward more relevant and effective output.

For example, instead of asking DALL-E to simply generate an image of a house, users should try something like one of the following five examples:

1. "Create an illustration of a modern, eco-friendly house nestled in a lush forest, with large windows and a minimalist design."

2. "Design a cozy cottage-style house with a sloping roof and a wraparound porch, surrounded by beautiful gardens and a tranquil lake."

See Figure 8.2 for the results of this prompt in DALL-E.

FIGURE 8.2. Image generated by DALL-E from the prompt "Design a cozy cottage-style house with a sloping roof and a wraparound porch, surrounded by beautiful gardens and a tranquil lake."

3. *"Imagine a futuristic smart house with sleek lines, cutting-edge technology, and an abundance of natural light, set against a backdrop of a bustling city skyline."*

4. *"Illustrate a charming Victorian-era house with intricate gables, a wrap-around porch, and a picket fence, surrounded by a quaint town square and historic buildings."*

5. *"Create an image of a sustainable, off-grid cabin nestled in a rugged mountain landscape, with a natural stone facade, solar panels, and a composting toilet."*

USE A CONSISTENT TONE AND STYLE

Consistency in tone and style is important for creating a cohesive and engaging piece of content. Users should maintain the same tone and style throughout their prompts to ensure that the generated content aligns with their brand's voice and personality. This includes:

- **Language:** Using the same words, phrases, and sentences to convey your desired tone and style.

- **Tone:** Maintaining a consistent emotional tone, such as serious, playful, or professional, throughout all prompts.

- **Style:** Consistently using a specific writing style, such as descriptive, narrative, or expository, to convey information and elicit responses from the AI.

- **Format:** Using a consistent format for prompts, such as starting each prompt with a specific phrase or using a standardized template.

Consistency in tone and style helps establish a clear and recognizable voice that can guide the AI in producing content that aligns with the desired tone and style. It also makes it easier for the AI to understand and interpret prompts, leading to more accurate and relevant responses.

TEST AND REFINE

As with any marketing strategy, it's important to test and refine prompts over time to optimize their effectiveness. It's advisable to experiment with different phrasing, tone, and style to find what works best for each specific use case.

Similar to how one becomes successful in other areas of their work, it is important to try different approaches and methods to see what generates the best results. Users should try different approaches to prompt writing and keep a record of the prompts they have used that have yielded good results. It might be possible to reuse the structure and even some of the language from those prompts again and again.

Additionally, one may find the specific AI-based tools yield better results for different types of tasks. For instance, when dealing with images, a user might find a favorite tool for generating brand new images (e.g., Midjourney or DALL-E), while preferring to work with a legacy image editing application (e.g., Adobe Photoshop or Canvas) for some graphics work involving designs or images they already created.

USE A COMBINATION OF PROMPTS AND INPUT VARIABLES

Depending on the specific use case, one may want to combine prompts with input variables to generate more tailored and relevant content.

When someone wants to generate a list of product features for a new smartphone, they have a set of input variables that describe the phone's specifications, such as screen size, camera resolution, and battery life. It's also practical to include some creative elements in the product description, such as a catchy tagline or a memorable slogan.

In this case, using a combination of prompts and input variables can help generate a more comprehensive and engaging list of product features. Here's an example of what the prompt might look like:

```
Write a list of product features for our new smartphone,
including both technical specifications and creative
elements that capture the phone's unique value proposition.
Input variables include screen size, camera resolution,
battery life, and tagline. The list should be engaging,
informative, and highlight the phone's key benefits.

Input Variables:

* Screen size: 6.5 inches
* Camera resolution: 12 megapixels
* Battery life: All-day battery with fast charging capabilities
* Tagline: "Capture life in stunning detail"
```

By combining the input variables with the prompt, it's possible to generate a list of product features that not only list the technical specifications but also includes creative elements that highlight the phone's unique value proposition and capture the user's attention. Here's an example of what the generated list might look like:

Our new smartphone boasts a stunning 6.5-inch screen, perfect for watching your favorite shows or playing games on the go. With a 12 megapixel camera, you can capture life in stunning detail and preserve memories that last a lifetime. And with our all-day battery and fast charging capabilities, you'll never miss a moment. Plus, our tagline 'Capture life in stunning detail' perfectly encapsulates the phone's unique value proposition—to experience life in high definition."

CONCLUSION

By following these guidelines, marketers can write more effective prompts in a generative AI tool to get higher quality and more efficient results, ultimately leading to better business outcomes and stronger brand engagement.

CHAPTER 9

GENERATIVE *AI* CASES AND *EXAMPLES*

With a better understanding of best practices to create prompts, it's time to go through some specific use cases, so readers can apply the principles that have been discussed to a broad array of marketing examples.

A hypothetical company and product will be used as an example, and readers will see how they can apply generative AI tools and proper prompt usage to generate great results for their marketing team.

The marketing campaign is for the fictional HomeSmart Pro platform. It is a smart home automation system that integrates with various devices such as thermostats, lighting, and security cameras. The target audience is tech-savvy homeowners who want to increase energy, efficiency, convenience, and home security.

GENERATING MARKETING AND ADVERTISING CONTENT

The following sections explore some best practices.

Strategies and Approaches

Before the process of generating copy begins, it's necessary to think through all of the possibilities to help market the HomeSmart Pro smart home automation system. Start by asking for some ideas of ways to reach our target audience of tech-savvy homeowners who want to increase energy efficiency, convenience and home security.

Asking, "What are some marketing strategies that would effectively market our HomeSmart Pro home automation product tech-savvy homeowners who want to increase energy efficiency, convenience and home security?" to a local copy of Meta's Lllama 2 large language model, produces the following result:

```
Potential Marketing Strategies for the HomeSmart Pro home
automation system include:

1.  Social media campaigns: Create engaging content
    showcasing the benefits of HomeSmart Pro, such as energy
    savings, improved home security, and seamless voice
    control. Use hashtags and influencer partnerships to
    increase brand visibility and reach a wider audience.
2.  Influencer marketing: Partner with tech-savvy influencers
    who can showcase the features and benefits of HomeSmart
    Pro in their own homes. This can help build credibility
    and trust among potential customers.
3.  Content marketing: Create informative blog posts,
    videos, and infographics that highlight the technical
    specifications and features of HomeSmart Pro. Use SEO
    techniques to ensure high search engine rankings and
    attract organic traffic.
4.  Email marketing: Send targeted email campaigns to
    potential customers who have shown interest in smart home
    automation systems. Offer exclusive promotions, discounts,
    or early access to new features to encourage conversion.
5.  Trade shows and events: Showcase HomeSmart Pro
    at relevant trade shows and events to reach a
    wider audience and generate leads. Offer product
    demonstrations and interactive experiences to engage
    potential customers.
```

While there was nothing groundbreaking here, if the current HomeSmart Pro marketing team didn't have trade shows and events on their radar, this could be beneficial.

As a comparison, the same prompt was fed to OpenAI's ChatGPT, and it gave the following ideas for marketing tactics:

```
1.  Educational Content and Workshops: Create and
    distribute content that educates your target audience
    on the benefits of smart home automation, focusing on
    energy savings, convenience, and security enhancements.
```

Workshops can be virtual or in-person, showcasing real-life applications and benefits.

2. *Partnerships with Eco-friendly and Tech Companies: Collaborate with companies that specialize in energy-efficient appliances, solar energy, and tech gadgets. These partnerships can lead to bundled offers or discounts for customers who integrate these products with the HomeSmart Pro platform.*

3. *Social Proof and Testimonials: Leverage reviews, testimonials, and case studies from current users who have seen tangible benefits from using HomeSmart Pro 2.0. Highlight these stories in your marketing campaigns to build trust and credibility.*

4. *Influencer and Blogger Collaborations: Partner with tech influencers and bloggers to showcase the HomeSmart Pro system in action. This can help reach a wider audience and tap into the followers of well-respected tech enthusiasts.*

5. *Interactive Online Demos: Offer potential customers the opportunity to explore the features of HomeSmart Pro 2.0 through interactive online demos or virtual home tours. This hands-on experience can help them visualize the system's benefits in their own homes.*

While there was some overlap between the two, it is interesting to see how two different LLMs can provide very different approaches and results. Users will want to compare different tools as well to see which work best for different needs.

Some other ways that generative AI could be even more beneficial might be to drill down on one of these ideas and ask for more potential ideas. For instance, if trade shows are something that is of interest to the HomeSmart Pro marketing team, they might ask generative AI for some ideas for branded giveaways for their booth, some ideas for product demos, and more.

Advertising Copy

Generative AI can be a great help for marketers that need to generate advertising copy for a variety of formats. Use the hypothetical HomeSmart Pro example, to create a few ad variations to sell the environmental energy efficiency benefits of the product. Start with a 30-second TV ad using the following prompt:

Write a script for a 30-second TV ad for the HomeSmart Pro 2.0 that focuses on the energy efficiency features of the product. Make sure to mention how the HomeSmart Pro 2.0 is the only product with patent-pending energy efficient software that maximizes efficiency while prioritizing the comfort of homeowners. End with a call to action to visit the HomeSmart Pro Web site to schedule a free consultation with a home automation professional.

Details regarding its patent-pending technology and a clear call to action were added. Here are the results from ChatGPT:

[Open with serene, uplifting music. Visuals of a sleek, modern home at dawn, lights turning on automatically.]

Narrator: "Welcome to a new day with HomeSmart Pro 2.0, where your home works smarter, not harder."

[Cut to a family enjoying breakfast. The thermostat adjusts in the background, lights dim to a morning glow.]

Narrator: "Introducing the only smart home system with patent-pending energy-efficient software, designed to maximize your home's efficiency..."

[Visual transition to a graph subtly showing energy use dropping, while the comfort level remains constant.]

Narrator: "...while always keeping your comfort in mind."

[Quick shots of the app in action: adjusting thermostat, turning off unused lights, closing blinds to keep the heat out.]

Narrator: "With HomeSmart Pro 2.0, saving energy is effortless. Our intelligent system ensures you're saving on bills without lifting a finger, making your home not just smart, but wise."

[End with the HomeSmart Pro logo, Web site URL displayed prominently.]

Narrator: "Step into the future of home automation. Visit the HomeSmart Pro Web site today to schedule your free consultation with a home automation professional. HomeSmart Pro 2.0 - Smart. Efficient. Home."

[The music fades out, leaving the viewer with the inviting image of the HomeSmart Pro interface on a mobile device, a cozy home in the background.]

[End of Ad]

Notice that in addition to the words to be spoken, ChatGPT took the prompt for a television ad and ensured that additional context such as an idea for the way that music and visuals should be used. Further refinements to this could adjust it to incorporate an urban setting versus a suburban one, or to show a single homeowner with a dog instead of a family. For now, leave this television ad as is, and move to another type of ad that needs to be created. This will be a print advertisement that goes inside the latest edition of the fictional *Smart Home Living* magazine. Create a new prompt specifically for this that builds on our previous request for a TV ad:

Now, write a 250 word advertisement to be placed in a print magazine for smart home enthusiasts that emphasizes the same product features that the TV ad did.

If the prompt is written in the same chat as the previous prompt for a TV ad, it will allow the user to benefit from everything already fed to ChatGPT, and they don't have to feed it everything from scratch again.

Here are the results:

(Headline) Transform Your Home into a Beacon of Efficiency with HomeSmart Pro 2.0

In the world of smart homes, efficiency and comfort often travel on parallel paths, rarely crossing. That was until HomeSmart Pro 2.0 redefined what it means to live smartly. As the only smart home automation system equipped with our exclusive, patent-pending energy-efficient software, HomeSmart Pro 2.0 is a game-changer for homeowners seeking the ultimate in energy savings without compromising on comfort.

Imagine a home that intuitively adapts to your lifestyle, conserving energy when you're away and ensuring a welcoming, comfortable environment when you're home. HomeSmart Pro 2.0 makes this a reality. Our innovative system seamlessly manages your home's lighting, temperature, and more, reducing your energy consumption and slashing your utility bills, all while maintaining the perfect living environment.

Why choose between saving the planet and living in comfort when you can do both? HomeSmart Pro 2.0 is not just a smart home system; it's a smarter way to live. Our technology is designed to learn from your habits, making real-time adjustments that optimize energy use without you ever noticing a difference—except when you see how low your energy bills can go.

Dive into the Future of Home Automation

Ready to elevate your home's intelligence and efficiency? Visit the HomeSmart Pro Web site today to schedule a free consultation with one of our home automation professionals. Discover how HomeSmart Pro 2.0 can transform your home into a model of smart living and energy efficiency.

HomeSmart Pro 2.0—Where Smart Meets Efficient.

The results did not specify any imagery for us, but we could refine our prompt to ask for that or other ideas as well. Additionally, we could keep going and ask for other types of ad variations such as any of the following:

- radio ads
- Google Search ad
- digital display ad
- Facebook or other social media ad

It's clear to see that the possibilities are nearly limitless, although to get the optimal results it is best to understand the unique specifications of each. As presented with the TV ad, ChatGPT did a good job of providing guidance on the overall flow of the ad, but some formats may be less familiar to the generative AI models.

Blog Post

An important component of any content marketing strategy is the creation of blog posts that can effectively speak to audiences about their potential challenges and the solutions that a product (like the HomeSmart Pro) can help solve. Create a blog post that touts some of the convenient features of the HomeSmart Pro version 2.0, that include automatically adjusting the thermostat to maintain a consistent temperature, as well as to turn off lights and other appliances when no one is in the room.

Target this post to a particular audience: busy professionals that work occasionally in the office and can have inconsistent schedules, making automation even more helpful within their hectic work-life balance.

Additionally, include a strong call to action (CTA) that drives readers to contact someone from the team for a free consultation.

Give ChatGPT the following prompt after first providing it a short amount of background information on the product:

Write a 800-1,000 word blog post about the convenience benefits of the HomeSmart Pro version 2.0 that is targeted at a busy professional that lives in the suburbs and commutes to the office 1-2 days a week. They have a hectic schedule which makes the automation features especially useful to them. These features include the ability to turn off lights and appliances when no one is in a room, as well as to maintain a constant temperature, or go into energy-saving mode when no one is home. End with a call to action to get a free consultation from a member of the HomeSmart Pro service team.

The following results are based on this prompt:

(Title) Unlocking the Ultimate Convenience with HomeSmart Pro 2.0: A Busy Professional's Dream

In today's fast-paced world, where every minute counts, busy professionals are constantly on the lookout for ways to streamline their daily routines and make their homes more efficient and comfortable. Enter HomeSmart Pro 2.0, the latest evolution in smart home automation, designed with the hectic lifestyle of the suburban commuter in mind. This innovative platform promises not just to enhance the convenience and comfort of your home but to transform it into a seamless, intuitive living experience.

(Subhead) Tailored Automation for the Busy Bee

Imagine leaving your home for the office on one of your in-office days, your mind already racing through the day's agenda. The last thing you want to worry about is whether you turned off all the lights, adjusted the thermostat, or unplugged unnecessary appliances. HomeSmart Pro 2.0 understands the rhythm of your unique lifestyle and automates these mundane tasks for you. With its advanced presence detection, the system knows when a room is no longer occupied, turning off lights and appliances to save energy without a second thought required from you.

But the convenience doesn't stop there. For those who appreciate coming home to the perfect environment, HomeSmart Pro 2.0 ensures your home's temperature is always just how you like it. On days you're at home, the system maintains your ideal comfort level. And when you're out, it effortlessly shifts into energy-saving mode, reducing your utility bills without sacrificing comfort, ready to welcome you back to a perfectly adjusted home.

(Subhead) A Personalized Experience

The true beauty of HomeSmart Pro 2.0 lies in its ability to learn and adapt to your schedule. Whether you're someone who commutes to the office 1-2 days a week or finds themselves frequently adjusting plans, the system's smart scheduling feature integrates with your calendar to anticipate your needs. It adjusts your home's settings in real-time, ensuring that no energy is wasted heating or cooling an empty house, yet always prioritizing your comfort when you're there.

Moreover, the platform's user-friendly interface allows you to customize settings to your heart's content, ensuring that every aspect of your home automation is tailored to fit your life perfectly. Whether it's setting specific lighting moods for different times of the day or ensuring your coffee machine turns on just as you're getting out of bed, HomeSmart Pro 2.0 makes it happen with the ease of a few clicks on your smartphone or voice commands to your smart assistant.

(Subhead) Security and Peace of Mind

For the busy professional, peace of mind is priceless, and HomeSmart Pro 2.0 delivers on this front as well. Beyond managing your home's energy use and comfort, the platform integrates with your home security system, offering you a comprehensive overview of your home's safety, no matter where you are. Receive real-time alerts and monitor your home directly from your smartphone, ensuring that you're always in the loop and your sanctuary is protected.

(Subhead) Embracing Sustainability

In an era where sustainability is increasingly becoming a priority for many, HomeSmart Pro 2.0 not only enhances the convenience of your home but also its energy efficiency. By optimizing the use of lights, appliances, and your HVAC system, the platform plays a crucial role in reducing your carbon footprint. It's a win-win, offering you the ultimate convenience while also doing your part for the planet.

(Subhead) The HomeSmart Pro 2.0 Promise

For the busy professional living in the suburbs, balancing a hectic schedule with the desire for a comfortable, efficient home, HomeSmart Pro 2.0 is more than just a smart home automation system—it's a lifestyle upgrade. It's about maximizing your time, energy, and resources, ensuring that you can focus on what truly matters, secure in the knowledge that your home is in good hands.

(Subhead) Ready to Transform Your Home?

If the idea of coming home to a perfectly comfortable, energy-efficient, and secure home appeals to you, it's time to consider HomeSmart Pro 2.0. Experience the ultimate convenience tailored to fit the busy, dynamic lifestyle of today's professional. Don't let the mundane tasks of everyday life consume your precious time and energy. Let

HomeSmart Pro 2.0 take care of your home, so you can take care of living your best life.

We invite you to reach out for a free consultation with a member of the HomeSmart Pro service team. Discover how HomeSmart Pro 2.0 can be customized to fit your life, your schedule, and your home. It's time to unlock the full potential of your home automation and step into a world of unmatched convenience and efficiency. Contact us today, and take the first step toward transforming your home into the smart, intuitive living space you deserve.

The prompt was followed to generate a blog post, although it's a good idea to do some further refinement, either within the ChatGPT interface itself, or in a separate editor. For instance, even though ChatGPT was to focus on the convenience aspects, the blog posts talk about security and energy efficiency benefits as well. That may be a little too much to cover for a single post, so some additional prompting to provide more details on the convenience features might be warranted.

Many marketers, however, are likely to take a starting point like this and make edits either in an editor like Microsoft Word or Google Docs, or directly in a Web site content management system (CMS) and then publish.

Web Site Copy

Similar to the blog post example, one may also want to create a supporting landing page on the Web site for an audience like the busy professionals for whom the blog post was written.

In addition to considering things like brand voice, target audience, and product features, when writing for Web site copy it's important to consider the content areas available on the Web page that copy can be placed within, as well as any graphics or photos that may need to accompany them.

For this purpose, write a prompt that includes these considerations, such as the following:

Please write copy for a Web site landing page designed to market the HomeSmart Pro 2.0 to the busy professionals audiences. It should focus on all three core benefits of energy efficiency, convenient automation, and security. The Web site has the following copy areas: 1) Heading (20- 25 words), 2) Subheading (35-50 words), 3) Lead paragraph (2-3 sentences), 4) Quote from a customer (15-20 words), and a call to action to contact the sales team for a demo. Additionally, please provide 2 suggestions for supporting images for the page.

The formatting of the page was addressed, and it ideally follows the order of content fields in the *CMS*, as well as the total content needs for the page. Here are the results from ChatGPT:

Heading:

"Transform Your Home with HomeSmart Pro 2.0: Efficiency, Convenience, and Security Redefined"

Subheading:

"Designed for the busy professional, HomeSmart Pro 2.0 automates your home life, optimizing energy use, ensuring security, and providing unparalleled convenience at every turn."

Lead Paragraph:

"Embrace the future of home living with HomeSmart Pro 2.0, where cutting-edge technology meets everyday convenience. Tailored for those with a demanding lifestyle, this platform seamlessly integrates with your home, making energy efficiency, security, and automated comfort a reality, not just a promise."

Quote from a Customer:

"HomeSmart Pro 2.0 has revolutionized my daily routine. It's like having a personal assistant for my home!"

Call to Action:

"Ready to elevate your home experience? Contact our sales team now for a personalized HomeSmart Pro 2.0 demo and step into the future of smart living."

Suggestions for Supporting Images:

A Dynamic Home Dashboard: An image showcasing the HomeSmart Pro 2.0 user interface on a tablet or smartphone, displaying a sleek, easy-to-navigate dashboard that controls various aspects of the home, such as lighting, temperature, and security systems. This image would visually represent the ease and control that the platform offers to the user.

A Happy Family or Professional Relaxing at Home: A lifestyle image featuring a professional or a family comfortably relaxing in a living room that exemplifies a modern, smart home environment. The room should appear cozy and well-lit, with visible smart devices (like smart thermostats or lights) in action, subtly highlighting the comfort and convenience that HomeSmart Pro 2.0 brings into a home. This image would evoke the emotional benefits of a smart, automated home, appealing directly to the desires of the target audience for a harmonious work-life balance.

This same approach could be applied to other marketing content with strict requirements for copy areas, such as a marketing email, or even a print brochure or sell sheet.

Promotional Video Script

Videos can be effective tools to communicate with audiences that prefer more visual content while still enabling technical details and other information to be conveyed. To market the HomeSmart Pro system, give instructions to a local copy of Llama 2 and give it a detailed prompt.

Be sure to include several key components that are specific to videos content, as well as to make sure that the generative AI tool understands the purpose and focus of the video, which is to highlight the energy efficiency features of the product. Describe the target audience for the video, and for this one pick suburban home dwellers that live in areas in which the weather fluctuates greatly between hot and cold.

It also helps to provide a basic outline of the video, as well as the target length for each section. In this case, there is a short, two-minute video with a brief introduction and conclusion, and the middle of the video focuses on the energy efficiency features.

At this point, one can assume that the AI tool has some basic background on the product, such as the high-level overview provided earlier in this chapter.

The prompt is the following:

Provide me a 2-minute video script for an explainer video that demonstrates the energy efficiency features of the SmartHome Pro. These features include the following:

The product can be automated to turn off when no one is in a room the system can adjust the thermostats in the home based on the weather conditions outside, such as if it is a sunny or cloudy day as well as the temperature the system is able to automatically adjust based on daily routines. The video should include a brief introduction (15-20 seconds) touting the overall benefits of the product and conclude (15-20 seconds) with a recap of the energy efficiency features.

The script should be written from the point of view of a homeowner in the suburbs in a climate that fluctuates between hot summers and cold often snowy winters.

It's clear to see the considerations mentioned above were addressed, and there are several points of guidance to make sure the script will be close to expectations. The output for the script from Llama 2 is the following:

Intro (15-20 seconds):

"Are you tired of wasting money on your energy bills? Do you want to reduce your carbon footprint and live more sustainably? Look no further than the SmartHome Pro! This revolutionary system will transform your home into a smart, energy-efficient oasis. Say goodbye to high energy bills and hello to a more comfortable, eco-friendly living space."

Script (1 minute 45 seconds):

"As a homeowner in the suburbs, I know how important it is to keep my home comfortable and energy-efficient.

That's why I love the SmartHome Pro! With its advanced features, I can automate my home's lighting, temperature, and security with ease.

For example, did you know that the SmartHome Pro can automatically turn off lights and appliances when no one is in a room? This feature not only saves energy but also helps extend the lifespan of my devices. Plus, it's so easy to use - I just need to set up a few simple routines and let the system do the rest!

But that's not all - the SmartHome Pro can also adjust my thermostats based on the weather conditions outside. For instance, if it's a sunny day, the system will automatically lower the temperature to save energy. And if it's a cloudy day or cold winter night, the system will adjust the temperature accordingly to keep my home cozy and comfortable.

Perhaps the best part is that the SmartHome Pro learns my daily routines and adjusts the lighting, temperature, and security settings accordingly. For instance, if I usually watch TV in the living room at 7 PM, the system will automatically turn on the lights and adjust the temperature to my preferred setting. It's like having a personal butler for my home!

Conclusion (15-20 seconds):

"So why wait? Upgrade to the SmartHome Pro today and start enjoying the benefits of energy efficiency, convenience, and peace of mind. Say goodbye to high energy bills and hello to a more sustainable, comfortable living space. Get ready to love your home - and the planet - just a little bit more."

Note: The script should be tailored to the specific product features and target audience, and can be adjusted based on the desired video length and tone.

Of course, the first draft produced from generative AI is rarely if ever perfect, and it can also help users understand where more information or detail needs to be provided. For instance, in the previous prompt, there was no mention that the HomeSmart Pro is now in a new and improved version 2.0, which will be helpful to tout in the video. Also, after showing this script to the marketing team, it was agreed that the video should start off a little friendlier.

So, to do this, instead of writing the prompt from scratch again, it will be refined with the following prompt:

Please rewrite the script with a friendlier tone, and mention that SmartHome Pro is now in a new and improved version 2.0

Some may find it helpful to go into some details about what exactly is "new" and "improved" in version 2.0, but for the purposes of this example we kept it pretty simple. As a result, here is how the script was rewritten:

Intro (15-20 seconds):

"Hey there! Are you tired of wasting money on your energy bills? Do you want to reduce your carbon footprint and live more sustainably? Well, say no more! I've got the perfect solution for you—the SmartHome Pro version 2.0!

Script (80-90 seconds):

As a homeowner in the suburbs, I know how important it is to keep my home comfortable and energy-efficient.

That's why I love the SmartHome Pro! With its advanced features, I can automate my home's lighting, temperature, and security with ease. Plus, with version 2.0, I get even more awesome features that make my life easier and my home even more eco-friendly!

For example, did you know that the SmartHome Pro can automatically turn off lights and appliances when no one is in a room? This feature not only saves energy but also helps extend the lifespan of my devices. Plus, it's so easy to use - I just need to set up a few simple routines and let the system do the rest!

But that's not all—the SmartHome Pro can also adjust my thermostats based on the weather conditions outside. For instance, if it's a sunny day, the system will automatically lower the temperature to save energy. And if it's a cloudy day or cold winter night, the system will adjust the temperature accordingly to

keep my home cozy and comfortable.

Perhaps the best part is that the SmartHome Pro learns my daily routines and adjusts the lighting, temperature, and security settings accordingly. For instance, if I usually watch TV in the living room at 7PM, the system will automatically turn on the lights and adjust the temperature to my preferred setting. It's like having a personal butler for my home!

Conclusion (15-20 seconds):

So why wait? Upgrade to the SmartHome Pro version 2.0 today and start enjoying the benefits of energy efficiency, convenience, and peace of mind. Say goodbye to high energy bills and hello to a more sustainable, comfortable living space. Get ready to love your home—and the planet—just a little bit more."

Readers will notice immediately a less formal tone, plus the mention of the 2.0 version at the beginning and end of the video. Additionally, the previous instructions about the length and outline remained intact. This means that the script, or even portions of it could continue to be refined indefinitely until it is ready to be shared.

Social Media Organic and Advertising Posts

Brand consistency is also important when communicating across channels, including social media channels. Thus, the Jasper marketing tool was used to generate several social media posts as part of a campaign. The prompt given was taken from earlier in this chapter:

Prompt:

The HomeSmart Pro platform is a smart home automation system that integrates with various devices such as thermostats, lighting, and security cameras. The target audience is tech-savvy homeowners who want to increase energy, efficiency, convenience, and home security.
We are planning a launch campaign for the product and need social media posts and other marketing content to help promote it.

Using this as a prompt, it generated the following samples:

LinkedIn Post:

Hello LinkedIn Network,

I am thrilled to share an innovation that has been making waves in the world of home automation—the HomeSmart Pro platform. Imagine being able to control your home's thermostat, lighting, and security cameras all from one place, seamlessly integrated for maximum efficiency? That's the power of HomeSmart Pro! 🏠💡

To the tech-savvy homeowners who value convenience, energy efficiency, and security, this is the solution you've been waiting for. The HomeSmart Pro not only offers you a way to customize your home environment to your liking, but also ensures you can do so in the most energy-efficient manner. This means saving on your utility bills without compromising on your comfort or safety.

But the innovation doesn't stop there. With HomeSmart Pro, you are able to monitor and control your home from anywhere, anytime. Whether you're at work, on vacation, or simply in another room, peace of mind is right at your fingertips.

The value proposition of HomeSmart Pro extends beyond just the convenience and cost-effectiveness. As we become more conscious of our impact on the environment, this platform provides a powerful tool to reduce our energy consumption and carbon footprint. It's a win-win situation—for you, and for Mother Earth. 🌍💚

To wrap up, HomeSmart Pro is more than just a smart home automation system. It's a lifestyle choice—one that combines comfort, security, energy efficiency, and environmental consciousness.

To my fellow professionals, I challenge you to embrace this innovation and enhance your living experience. Let's redefine what it means to be a homeowner in the 21st century. Join me and let's make our homes smarter, together!

#HomeSmartPro #SmartLiving

Tweet Ideas:

1. "Control your world from the palm of your hand with #HomeSmartPro. It's not just smart, it's genius! 💡🍞🌡 #SmartHome"

2. "Lighting, heating, security cameras... What if you could manage them all from one app? Welcome to #HomeSmartPro. 🏠💡🍞 #HomeAutomation"

3. "Cut those energy bills down to size with #HomeSmartPro. It's not just a smart home, it's a wise investment. 💰🌍 #EnergyEfficient"

4. "Maximize convenience and control with #HomeSmartPro. Because your home should work for you, not the other way around. 🏠👍 #SmartLiving"

5. "Never worry about leaving the lights on again. With #HomeSmartPro, home is where the tech is. 💡📲 #SmartHome #EcoFriendly"

6. "Got a minute? That's all it takes to secure your home with #HomeSmartPro. Peace of mind, at your fingertips. 🏠🍞 #HomeSecurity"

7. "The future called. It wants its smart home back. Get ahead of the curve with #HomeSmartPro. 🏠💡🍞 #LifeAutomated"

8. *"Turn your home into a fortress of efficiency with #HomeSmartPro. Because being smart should always feel this good. 💡🪙 #EnergySavings"*

9. *"Wake up, coffee's ready. Arrive home, lights on. Leave, security engaged. Welcome to life with #HomeSmartPro. 🏠💡🍰 #SmartLiving"*

10. *"The smart choice for smart homeowners. Elevate your living with #HomeSmartPro. Because your home deserves the best. 🏠💡🍞 #HomeAutomation"*

Facebook Image Ad

Primary Text: Upgrade your home with HomeSmart Pro! Control lights, temperature, and security all from one place.

Headline: Smart Home, Smarter Living

Description: Enhance efficiency and security today.

The preceding examples show that, based on the level of detail we provided in a prompt, the tool was able to generate some posts that could be compelling to the target audiences. What also might be noticeable, however, is that the specifics on the product are sparse, which means that a more effective set of outputs may require additional training on product specifics, competitive advantages, or other information that can help the ads to feel more specific both to the product as well as to how they can help solve the specific needs of the audience.

DATA ANALYSIS

So far in this chapter, there has been a reliance on text prompts to generate primarily text-based outputs. Depending on the generative AI tools used, there can be varying levels of training performed to help ensure accurate responses.

Following is information about using generative AI to analyze and understand data sets, and for this some tools, as well as some sample data sets will be made available for download so readers can try out some of these techniques.

Research

Following is an example that will provide some of the strengths of generative AI as well as some of its limitations. For instance, the goal is to understand consumer behavior in regard to cola consumption and how it has shifted. The work is primarily focused on the United States, so there is no point in looking at global trends, which likely vary from region to region. Using ChatGPT, enter the following prompt:

I am doing research on soft drink consumption in the United States. Can you give me information on how many consumers drink Coca-Cola versus Pepsi, and how this has changed over the last 10 years that you have data available?

Note that the prompt included some context: that the purpose of this question is to do research, as well as being focused on the United States. Researchers also want to look at trends versus a single year, so it was phrased hoping that up to a decade of data is available.

ChatGPT's response is below:

As of my last update in April 2023, I don't have the specific, up-to-date figures for Coca-Cola and Pepsi consumption over the past decade. However, I can provide some general insights into the trends and factors that have influenced soft drink consumption in the United States, particularly focusing on these two major brands.

Market Share and Consumer Preferences

Historical Dominance: Coca-Cola and Pepsi have long been dominant players in the soft drink market, often engaged in what's popularly known as the "Cola Wars." Historically, Coca-Cola has usually held a larger share of the market compared to Pepsi, but both brands have enjoyed a loyal customer base.

Shifts in Consumption Patterns: Over the past decade, there has been a noticeable shift in consumer preferences, with a growing trend toward healthier lifestyles. This has impacted the sales of traditional sugary sodas, as consumers increasingly opt for healthier alternatives like water, flavored water, and nonsugar sweetened beverages.

Innovation and Diversification: Both companies have responded to changing consumer tastes by diversifying their product lines to include low-sugar, zero-sugar, and diet options, as well as venturing into noncarbonated beverages like teas, juices, and bottled waters. The success of these new products has influenced their market shares and consumer preferences.

Market Trends and Data

Market Research Reports: To get precise and current figures on the consumption of Coca-Cola versus Pepsi, one would typically refer to market research reports from firms like Nielsen, IBISWorld, or Euromonitor. These reports provide detailed analyses of market shares, consumer behavior, and brand preferences.

Consumer Surveys and Studies: Surveys and longitudinal studies can offer insights into consumer preferences, brand loyalty, and the reasons behind the choice of one brand over another. These studies might reveal demographic trends, such as preferences varying by age group, region, or socioeconomic status.

Impact of Marketing and Branding: The marketing strategies and branding efforts of both companies have significantly influenced consumer preferences. Analyzing the impact of their advertising campaigns, sponsorships, and social media presence can provide insights into their popularity and consumer engagement.

Recent Developments

Health and Wellness Trends: The increasing consumer focus on health and wellness continues to shape the industry, with both companies expanding their portfolios to include healthier options and responding to the demand for transparency in labeling and the reduction of artificial ingredients.

Sustainability and Ethical Concerns: Consumer preferences are also increasingly influenced by the companies' commitments to sustainability, ethical sourcing, and

environmental responsibility, which can impact brand
loyalty and consumption choices.

To obtain the most recent and specific data on the
consumption rates of Coca-Cola versus Pepsi, I recommend
accessing the latest industry reports, company financial
statements, and consumer research studies. These documents
often require a subscription or purchase but can provide
the most accurate and detailed insights into current trends
and future projections in the soft drink market.

There are a few things to note about the response. First, the prompt didn't specify the output format, so ChatGPT defaulted to writing prose versus supplying data in some type of tabular format.

Second, there is a caveat given about the recency (at the beginning) as well as the accuracy (at the end) of the information.

Yes, despite this, there is a good deal of helpful information for a marketer wishing to do research on consumer behavior in this area. It is possible that a query for data that is made publicly available might have yielded a more quantitative response, and that is something it would be recommended that users try.

Customer Retention Strategies

Next, generate a sample data set, and then use it to see how generative AI can help predict customer churn, or the likelihood that a customer will stop buying from the researcher's company and switch to a competitor.

To start, generate a sample data set by using a simple prompt in ChatGPT:

Please generate a data set for me in tabular format that
includes 50 rows of information that fits the following
format: 1) "User Name" which is populated in each row by
a randomly generated human name, 2) "Last purchase date"
which is populated in each row by a randomly generated
date between January 1, 2022 and December 31, 2023, 3)
"Number of Customer Service Inquiries" which is a randomly
generated number between 1 and 10, and 4) "Number of total

purchases" which is populated by a randomly generated
number between 1 and 5.

The actual data will likely be more complex, but for this sample exercise, simplify to just four fields. Following is the sample dataset that ChatGPT generated based on that prompt:

User Name	Last Purchase Date	Number of Customer Service Inquiries	Number of Total Purchases
Avery Johnson	2022-03-15	3	2
Jordan Ellis	2023-11-28	6	1
Taylor Green	2022-07-22	2	5
Morgan Carter	2023-01-09	7	3
Casey Bailey	2022-05-18	4	2
Riley Ford	2023-08-14	1	4
Cameron Lee	2022-11-30	5	1
Alex Smith	2023-07-03	8	5
Jamie Lopez	2022-02-09	3	3
Jordan Davis	2023-12-17	6	2
Casey White	2022-08-26	2	1
Taylor Brown	2023-05-19	9	4
Morgan Martinez	2022-04-13	5	5
Avery Wilson	2023-02-27	4	2
Riley Thompson	2022-09-05	1	3
Jordan Anderson	2023-10-21	7	1
Jamie Moore	2022-06-11	3	4
Casey Clark	2023-03-30	8	5
Alex Rodriguez	2022-12-24	2	2
Cameron Walker	2023-09-12	6	1
Taylor Harris	2022-01-20	5	3
Morgan Young	2023-06-07	9	4
Avery King	2022-10-16	4	5
Riley Gonzalez	2023-04-05	1	2
Jordan Scott	2022-03-28	7	1
Casey Evans	2023-11-15	3	3
Alex Wright	2022-07-05	8	4

User Name	Last Purchase Date	Number of Customer Service Inquiries	Number of Total Purchases
Cameron Johnson	2023-01-12	2	5
Taylor Martin	2022-05-21	6	2
Morgan Jackson	2023-08-19	1	1
Avery Lee	2022-11-02	5	3
Riley Hernandez	2023-07-10	9	4
Jordan King	2022-02-14	3	5
Casey Wright	2023-12-05	4	2
Alex Lopez	2022-08-31	7	1
Cameron Hill	2023-05-24	2	3
Taylor Clark	2022-04-19	8	4
Morgan Adams	2023-03-03	5	5
Avery Thompson	2022-09-12	1	2
Riley Martinez	2023-10-28	6	1
Jordan White	2022-06-17	3	3
Casey Gonzalez	2023-04-15	8	4
Alex Clark	2022-12-29	4	5
Cameron Allen	2023-09-05	2	2
Taylor Robinson	2022-01-27	7	1
Morgan Kim	2023-06-14	5	3
Avery Hernandez	2022-10-23	9	4
Riley Williams	2023-04-12	3	5
Jordan Martinez	2022-03-20	6	2
Casey Lee	2023-11-22	4	1

As you can see, the data produced precisely what was requested: four columns with a name, date of last purchase, a number of customer service complaints, and total number of purchases.

Now, create a simple formula that will be used to predict churn. Again, the company will likely have more data to work with and a more complex model, but for the purposes of this exercise, assume the following: a high likelihood of churn equals a customer that has a high level of customer service complaints and the most time elapsing since their last purchase.

With this in mind, give ChatGPT the following prompt:

Using the data in the table, please re-order the customers according to their likelihood to churn with the most likely first. The greatest likelihood to churn will be those customers with the highest number of customer service inquiries (column 3) and the most time elapsed since their last purchase, based on today's date (2024-02-29), with additional weighting for customers that have a higher number of total purchases.

Following is ChatGPT's response to the prompt, which includes both a description of the rationale, as well as the reordered dataset:

To reorder the customers based on their likelihood to churn, we'll consider the following factors:

1. *Number of Customer Service Inquiries: Higher numbers suggest potential dissatisfaction or issues, increasing churn likelihood.*
2. *Time Elapsed Since Last Purchase: The longer the time since the last purchase, the higher the chance the customer has churned or will churn.*
3. *Number of Total Purchases: More purchases might indicate higher engagement or more opportunities for dissatisfaction, influencing churn risk.*

Given these criteria and today's date (2024-02-29), we'll sort the customers, prioritizing them by the number of customer service inquiries first, then by the elapsed time since their last purchase, and finally considering the number of total purchases. The exact calculation for churn likelihood isn't provided, so we'll use these factors qualitatively to rank the customers.

Here's the reordered list, starting with those most likely to churn:

User Name	Last Purchase Date	Number of Customer Service Inquiries	Number of Total Purchases
Taylor Harris	2022-01-20	9	3
Riley Hernandez	2023-07-10	9	4
Morgan Young	2023-06-07	9	4
Avery Hernandez	2022-10-23	9	4
Casey Evans	2023-11-15	8	3
Alex Wright	2022-07-05	8	4
Casey Gonzalez	2023-04-15	8	4
Casey Clark	2023-03-30	8	5
Taylor Martin	2022-05-21	6	2
Cameron Hill	2023-05-24	6	3
Riley Martinez	2023-10-28	6	1
Jordan Davis	2023-12-17	6	2
Jordan Martinez	2022-03-20	6	2
Alex Smith	2023-07-03	8	5
Taylor Clark	2022-04-19	8	4
Morgan Carter	2023-01-09	7	3
Alex Lopez	2022-08-31	7	1
Jordan Anderson	2023-10-21	7	1
Taylor Robinson	2022-01-27	7	1
Jordan Scott	2022-03-28	7	1
Cameron Walker	2023-09-12	6	1
Jamie Moore	2022-06-11	3	4
Avery King	2022-10-16	4	5
Morgan Adams	2023-03-03	5	5
Casey Wright	2023-12-05	4	2
Avery Lee	2022-11-02	5	3
Morgan Jackson	2023-08-19	1	1
Cameron Johnson	2023-01-12	2	5
Jordan Ellis	2023-11-28	6	1
Riley Ford	2023-08-14	1	4
Avery Wilson	2023-02-27	4	2
Jamie Lopez	2022-02-09	3	3

User Name	Last Purchase Date	Number of Customer Service Inquiries	Number of Total Purchases
Casey Lee	2023-11-22	4	1
Cameron Lee	2022-11-30	5	1
Alex Clark	2022-12-29	4	5
Avery Johnson	2022-03-15	3	2
Riley Williams	2023-04-12	3	5
Morgan Martinez	2022-04-13	5	5
Taylor Brown	2023-05-19	9	4
Casey Bailey	2022-05-18	4	2
Riley Thompson	2022-09-05	1	3
Cameron Allen	2023-09-05	2	2
Taylor Green	2022-07-22	2	5
Casey White	2022-08-26	2	1
Alex Rodriguez	2022-12-24	2	2
Jamie Lopez	2022-02-09	3	3
Jordan King	2022-02-14	3	5

This reordered list prioritizes customers most likely to churn, based on the provided criteria. It's important to note that this is a qualitative assessment, as the exact churn likelihood would require a more sophisticated model, possibly incorporating more detailed customer interaction data and behavioral analytics.

There are a few things to note regarding the response from ChatGPT. First, while Microsoft Excel or a spreadsheet tool could have helped sort this simple list of information, transformation of this table of information was possible by asking a few simple questions, and if the dataset included many more columns it would increase the complexity of using a tool like Excel to do so.

Second, ChatGPT provided a rationale for what it did. It mirrored the prompt, but it is still important that there is transparency in how it approached the analysis. This could also help adjust calculations if needed in the future.

Finally, ChatGPT provided a caveat about the accuracy of the data and a recommendation of how it could be improved. This could be helpful to teams that are trying to perform quick assessments yet need a more accurate method of measurement.

That said, one can see the power of generative AI to analyze datasets quickly and without expert knowledge of an additional application.

CONCLUSION

This information has only just scratched the surface of the potential of using generative AI with these examples, but hopefully readers can see the possibilities that AI-based approaches can have for the work of marketing teams.

PART IV

INTEGRATION AND OPTIMIZATION OF AI AND MARKETING

This last part of the book explores how AI can be meaningfully applied to marketing using some of the categories discussed in the previous three parts. This will be looked at in a few ways, from the mindset and cultural shifts, to how to think of the business implications of greater strategic adoption of artificial intelligence. The text also explores a critical topic, which is the bias that can skew the effectiveness and fairness of the work done with artificial intelligence. Finally, there is information about the adoption of AI in marketing with an iterative approach utilizing continuous improvement methods.

Every organization is different. Still, the focus will stay on the areas where businesses across industries and even sizes may share common needs, challenges, and opportunities. In general, some of the ideas may lend themselves more to larger companies, though even a small company or start-up can apply some of this advice later in its growth stages.

CHAPTER 10

THE AI ADOPTION MINDSET

As with any technology shift, the platforms or technologies themselves are often the least disruptive aspect to businesses. Instead, the "people" part of the three-legged stool of "people, process, and platforms" can make or break an initiative. Because of this, it is important that leaders and teams have the right mindset when considering the greater adoption of AI-based solutions.

In this chapter, the focus will not be on specific AI tools but instead talk about the mindset shift teams should have as they either slowly or quickly embrace artificial intelligence in their work. The following presents four ways to do this.

AUGMENTATION, NOT REPLACEMENT

First, a good way of thinking about artificial intelligence is that it is best utilized as augmentation for people and not as a replacement for them. After all, what percentage of a team's work, on average, is monotonous and could conceivably be automated? According to a recent survey by UIPath [UIP22], a little over two thirds (67%) of workers in the United States feel that tasks that could easily be automated fill much of their day.[1] While it may go without saying, according to Jennifer Moss in her article in *Harvard Business Review* [MOSS20], workplace monotony can directly impact employee morale, quality of work, and performance.[2]

Thus, there is an opportunity here for new solutions. Employees want to be freed up from monotonous, repetitive tasks, and doing so with AI-based tools can allow teams to focus on more valuable, strategic work. This could include innovations that improve the customer experience, save the company money, or bring in new sources of revenue, all while AI is taking care of the drudgery. It's a win-win.

STARTING, NOT FINISHING

A second good approach to utilizing artificial intelligence in a team's work is that it can be a great starting point but should not be depended upon to complete a strategic brief, plan, or anything else.

For instance, ChatGPT and other generative AI tools offer great starting points for just about any marketing task or initiative one might be assigned. By asking a series of questions, one can get some basic ideas and information on which to build a report, an article, or other more strategic outputs. This is utilizing technology so that every party is playing to their strengths. For all their benefits, humans often have a hard time starting things, as evidenced by their tendency to procrastinate. This reluctance to start can be negated by utilizing AI tools to build out instead of staring at a blank screen and waiting for inspiration to come.

Thus, thinking of AI as a starting point and strategic human teammates as the closers can help to frame some more successful adoption of artificial intelligence in an organization.

CURATION, NOT SUMMARIZATION

The third way to think about adopting AI into one's work is that it can be a great curator of information for individuals and their teams, given its ability to crawl the entire internet looking for ideas, information, and insights. That said, although tools like ChatGPT and others can find information and summarize it from across the Web, this approach has some fairly serious downsides.

For one, it can often be difficult to determine exactly where some of the information is being summarized from. It may be from a less-than-reputable source, or it may be from an edge case that is not fully representative of the information you are attempting to summarize.

Additionally, there can be elements of bias that are difficult to detect and protect against if one relies on AI to scour the Web for any and all information on a topic.

Thus, people can use AI-based technologies to curate a wealth of information that humans can then review and ensure meet the standards and focus they seek. This leverages the strength of AI to scour large troves of information while leaving humans to make high-level judgments about what is appropriate and what is not.

ANALYSIS, NOT STRATEGY

Finally, AI-based technologies like machine learning, deep learning, and natural language processing (NLP) can help teams analyze large amounts of data that humans simply could not in any reasonable manner. This can be a building block as teams are brought in to take that analysis by AI and build strategies and plans that benefit from AI's ability to parse vast amounts of structured and unstructured data.

Similar to what was mentioned in the last point, it is best not to underestimate the ability for bias to be introduced into a machine learning algorithm. Strive for transparency in AI models so that bias can be rooted out and a team's strategies can be based on the best possible combination of machine and human intelligence. Bias will be discussed a little bit more in Chapters 11 and 12.

When teams approach AI realistically and with the mindset described in this chapter, leaders and teams can have incredible success while retaining the strategic control that humans are simply better at wielding.

NOTES

1 [UIP22] UIPath. "New UIPatch Study Reveals Half of Office Workers Willing to Resign from Their Jobs as Global Labor Shortage Amplifies Employee Burnout." UI Path. May 3, 2022. Retrieved March 4, 2023 from https://www.uipath.com/newsroom/new-uipath-study-reveals-half-of-office-workers-seeking-resignation.

2 [MOSS20] Moss, Jennifer. "If You're Burning Out, Carve a New Path." *Harvard Business Review*. April 1, 2020. Retrieved March 4, 2023 from https://hbr.org/2020/04/if-youre-burning-out-carve-a-new-path.

CHAPTER 11

HOW AI CHANGES YOUR MARKETING APPROACH

I t's hard to miss the consistent and continual stream of news and information about artificial intelligence (AI)-based applications and how they are predicted to change how we do business fundamentally. Their impact on marketing teams, processes, and platforms is transforming the way businesses operate. AI can automate mundane tasks like customer segmentation and campaign optimization while providing deeper insights into consumer behavior that were previously impossible to uncover. By leveraging AI's predictive capabilities, marketers can develop more targeted campaigns that drive better results for their organizations.

This chapter will discuss how successfully adopting AI within your marketing practice areas can have a meaningful impact on how you work. We'll look at this by focusing on three areas: your people, processes, and platforms.

HOW AI CHANGES YOUR MARKETING TEAMS

While it can be easy to think of artificial intelligence as something that could *replace* jobs or team members, a more accurate (and less scary) way of thinking about it is that AI can *augment* the work that great team members are already doing.

AI can be used to improve marketing teams by providing more accurate insights into customer behavior and preferences, thus focusing your people on what people do best: making strategic decisions based on the best possible information at hand. By leveraging machine learning algorithms, marketers can identify patterns in customer data that would have otherwise gone unnoticed. With this newfound understanding of their customers, marketers can create more effective campaigns tailored specifically for their audiences. AI also enables marketers to automate certain tasks, such as lead scoring and segmentation, freeing up time for other activities like content creation or strategic planning.

Thus, your teams can greatly benefit from AI-based applications, helping them perform higher-performing and more rewarding tasks by eliminating repetitive work and focusing them on the high-impact strategic areas that people do better in than machines.

For instance, here are several repetitive tasks that many marketers do on a daily or weekly basis that AI can now be used to help with:

1. **Data entry:** Marketers often spend time entering data into spreadsheets, databases, or other tools. AI can automate data entry tasks, such as extracting information from emails, Web sites, or social media platforms, and inputting it into a database or spreadsheet.

2. **Social media monitoring:** Marketers may spend hours each day monitoring social media for brand mentions, engaging with customers, and responding to messages. AI can help automate these tasks by using natural language processing (NLP) to identify relevant posts, comments, and direct messages, and then responding to them automatically.

3. **Email management:** Marketers often spend time composing, sending, and tracking emails. AI can help automate email management tasks, such as composing personalized emails, scheduling emails to send at optimal times, and tracking open rates, click-through rates, and conversion rates.

4. **Content creation:** Marketers may spend hours creating content for social media, blogs, or other platforms. AI can help automate content creation tasks by generating high-quality content based on a set of input variables, such as keywords, topics, and tone.

5. **Lead qualification:** Marketers often spend time qualifying leads based on criteria such as demographics, firmographic characteristics, or behavioral patterns. AI can help automate lead qualification tasks by using machine learning algorithms to identify high-quality leads and prioritize them for human follow-up.

6. **Customer segmentation:** Marketers may spend time segmenting customers based on criteria such as demographics, purchase history, or engagement levels. AI can help automate customer segmentation tasks by using clustering algorithms to group customers into distinct segments based on their characteristics and behaviors.

7. **Campaign tracking:** Marketers often spend time tracking the performance of marketing campaigns across multiple channels, such as social media, email, or search advertising. AI can help automate campaign tracking tasks by using machine learning algorithms to identify patterns and trends in customer behavior and attribution.

8. **Sales forecasting:** Marketers may spend time forecasting sales based on historical data, market trends, and other factors. AI can help automate sales forecasting tasks by using machine learning algorithms to identify patterns and trends in customer behavior and predict future sales performance.

9. **Customer service:** Marketers often spend time responding to customer inquiries and providing support via email, chat, or other channels. AI can help automate customer service tasks by using NLP to identify common questions and provide automated responses, freeing up marketers' time for more strategic activities.

10. **Reporting and analytics:** Marketers may spend time creating reports and analyzing data to measure the performance of their campaigns and make data-driven decisions. AI can help automate reporting and analytics tasks by using machine learning algorithms to identify key metrics, track performance over time, and provide visualizations and insights that help marketers understand their results.

HOW AI CHANGES YOUR MARKETING PROCESSES

AI is also transforming marketing processes, making them faster and more efficient, with robotic process automation being one of the primary uses of artificial intelligence in business as a whole today. Thus, automating workflows can have an impact on your marketing team by eliminating the guesswork about the status of a particular campaign asset or deliverable.

AI can also improve external or customer-facing processes that involve customer communication. For example, AI-powered chatbots can take on simple sales or customer service requests and personalize responses based on the user's needs without needing real-time human input and more quickly get customers what they need. This frees up valuable time for marketing teams to focus on tasks that require human creativity, insights, and strategic decision-making. AI can also be used to automate processes like data analysis of multichannel campaigns or A/B testing, giving marketers access to insights on the effectiveness of their increasingly complex campaigns in real-time.

Whether internal or external-facing processes, artificial intelligence can enhance and improve your marketing and communications efforts. This creates cost-savings from more efficient work, improving your customer experience, increasing customer loyalty, and potentially contributing to greater customer lifetime value.

HOW AI CHANGES YOUR MARKETING PLATFORMS

Likely, some of the marketing platforms you use are already utilizing some type of AI functionality. This could range from basic algorithms to more complex machine-learning applications.

Over the months and years ahead, AI will continue revolutionizing marketing platforms by providing more accurate data and greater insights into customer behavior. By using machine learning algorithms within their platforms of choice, marketers can identify previously impossible patterns to uncover. This helps them create better segments for targeting and personalization, more compelling offers, and even campaigns, resulting in higher engagement and ROI with quicker turnaround times for gathering results. Additionally, AI-powered platforms can analyze large volumes of data quickly and accurately, enabling teams to launch campaigns faster than ever before.

Utilizing AI in your marketing platforms can give you the competitive edge you need as you battle for relevance, attention, and your customers' share of wallet.

CONCLUSION

Artificial intelligence is transforming how businesses operate, and its impact on marketing teams, processes, and platforms will only continue to grow. By continuing to leverage AI's predictive capabilities, marketers can develop more effective campaigns while freeing up valuable time and resources and ensuring they remain ahead of their competitors and maximize results for their organization. With the addition of generative AI, marketing teams can generate brand new content or variations of existing content. Thus, using multiple types of AI together can yield vast improvements to a marketing team's workflow, and the results of their work.

CHAPTER 12

WHEN AND WHERE TO INVEST IN AI

S o far, we have discussed several ways that artificial intelligence can help your organization's marketing efforts, as well as many that you're likely already relying on to power your current efforts. In fact, the adoption of AI within organizations continues to grow.

McKinsey's Global Survey on AI [MCK22] shows that, while the proportion of organizations using AI has remained relatively steady at between 50% and 60% for the past couple of years, the *amount* of uses they are engaging AI for has doubled between 2018 (1.9 average) and 2022 (3.8 uses).[1]

That said, as with any marketing technology investment, it is important to focus on the potential outcomes and if they will provide tangible benefits rather than simply chasing trends. The following sections pose four questions one should ask themselves and their team before making investment decisions in artificial intelligence-based technology.

IS IT SAVING TIME WHILE MAINTAINING OR INCREASING QUALITY?

The first question has two parts. As previously discussed, AI-driven tools have the potential to improve the targeting, personalization, and efficiency of marketing efforts, enhance customer insight and under-standing, and automate complex processes that used to require a lot of manual work. That all sounds pretty amazing, right?

What good is saving time on first drafts or creating reports more quickly if the quality of those drafts and reports takes more human effort to review and revise? In other words, despite AI's ability to provide a great starting point for work that marketers do or in report generation based on parsing a wide variety of statistics, the investment is only worth it if the work is streamlined while increasing quality.

Otherwise, AI-based tools are just making more work for the team. Thus, when using AI well, marketers can now make more informed decisions quickly, uncover new opportunities faster, and drive better results from their campaigns.

IS IT IMPROVING THE CUSTOMER EXPERIENCE?

As has been seen so far in this book, AI is a powerful tool that can be used to improve customer experience in many ways. The next question one should ask is will investing in artificial intelligence make such an improvement. This might be the key question one can ask themselves and their team.

The customer experience advantage from investments in AI are many-fold. AI-driven customer service bots can automate simple tasks and respond quickly to inquiries. In contrast, AI-driven products can personalize and customize services based on customer preferences, creating customized journeys based on propensity and next best action. Using AI, businesses can anticipate customer needs, provide personalized recommendations, and create tailored experiences for each user. This helps to drive engagement, loyalty, and better overall satisfaction for customers.

On the contrary, if a company's investment is simply using AI to mimic campaigns and experiences they are currently implementing with no noticeable improvement in their ability to target, personalize, and produce meaningful improvements, it is worth questioning whether the timing is right. While there is a lot of promise in using AI to improve the customer experience, make sure the enhancements are meaningful.

IS IT IMPROVING THE EMPLOYEE EXPERIENCE?

In addition to the points made earlier, there has been discussion about the customer experience in this book, which almost always refers to the end customer or the consumer who buys a company's products or services. But what about internal customers? After all, employees within an organization, such as the marketing department, are using the tools and applications that are implemented daily. When the right tools are matched with the right processes, this can majorly improve the employee experience. But when tools are cumbersome, when they introduce additional work or risk, or when they introduce unknowns into the equation, the results can be, at worst, more time-consuming than the tools they replaced, and, at best, they can lead to inconsistent performance, errors, and frequent oversights.

AI can help to improve the employee experience by automating mundane tasks, providing tailored job training and recommendations, and helping to eliminate human bias in decision-making processes. AI-powered tools can be used to detect potential areas of improvement in processes and operations, making it easier for employees to stay up-to-date on their skills and progress. Businesses can create a more productive, collaborative, and effective workplace by empowering employees with AI.

So, ask yourself if the tools you introduce will improve and augment your team's work or introduce new elements that cause risk and additional work.

IS IT EXPANDING YOUR INSIGHTS?

Finally, it's wise to look at AI investments in terms of what they can teach about customers and marketing efforts, focusing on continuous improvement. AI can be a powerful tool for gaining insights and analyzing customer behaviors and marketing campaigns, allowing marketers to monitor and analyze data related to customer engagement, purchasing habits, and preferences in real time. When used effectively, this helps to provide more granular and actionable insights that can be used to refine marketing strategies and improve customer experiences. AI-driven analysis tools can also identify trends in customer behaviors over time, enabling marketers to uncover valuable opportunities for growth and optimization.

AI can also enable the automation of manual processes, such as the tracking of sentiment across multiple channels, from social media posts to customer reviews. By leveraging natural language processing (NLP) technology, businesses can quickly monitor customer responses across different platforms and proactively address negative feedback or expand upon successes.

One should ask if an investment in AI will provide more meaningful insights or if it will simply provide more information to have to sift through to potentially find something valuable. If the former, it will allow for the development of better strategies for targeting customers with relevant ads that meet their needs. If the latter, AI can be beneficial by providing more data points to help one make decisions more quickly and efficiently.

CONCLUSION

As marketers use AI to gain insights and optimize their campaigns, they must be cautious to ensure it is not creating more work for them. AI should help to make processes and operations more efficient and effective, not add complexity or confusion to existing systems or even create additional layers of oversight, fact-checking, and rework.

Even in the best cases and the most robust applications, marketers must remember that AI can only provide so much insight and data-driven results; combining any findings with marketing expertise is important to develop the most successful strategies. Ultimately, AI should be used as a tool to enhance the effectiveness of marketers' existing efforts, streamline operations, and reduce time spent on manual tasks. By asking the four questions posed in this chapter, readers are more likely to make the right investment decisions.

NOTE

1   [MCK22] McKinsey. "The State of AI in 2022—and a Half Decade in Review." McKinsey & Company. December 6, 2022. Retrieved March 4, 2023 from https://www.mckinsey.com/capabilities/quantumblack/our-insights/the-state-of-ai-in-2022-and-a-half-decade-in-review.

CHAPTER 13

CHALLENGES OF AI

A s this book—as well as the countless other articles, interviews, and other materials of late have shown—AI holds plenty of promise for marketers, CX professionals, and many others in the business world. It is neither a silver bullet that can solve all challenges, nor is it flawless in its approaches to the tasks for which it is currently being utilized. In short, it's neither all good nor all bad, but still worth some strong considerations for usage in many areas.

This chapter explores a couple of the areas where a bit of realism is needed to temper the optimism and enthusiasm that has run rampant. Additionally, an important area will be examined—the bias that can be pervasive and destructive within artificial intelligence-based applications. This subject deserves attention in a mostly positive book about the topic of AI.

WHAT PEOPLE SHOULD AND SHOULDN'T EXPECT FROM AI

This book has talked about all of the amazing things that artificial intelligence can do for users and their marketing, but there is still plenty of work for the people out there. Humans are still good at a lot of things that machines are not.

Some sensational reports, such as one by McKinsey in 2017 [DIG23], illustrated that 30% of jobs would be replaced by automation and AI by 2030.[1] But this is only looking at one dimension of things. The World Economic Forum instead reported that AI will replace about eighty-five million jobs by the year 2025 but would also result in ninety-seven million new jobs being *created* by that same year [CIO23].[2] So the idea that we'll all be out of work due to AI is extremely misleading.

AUGMENTATION, NOT REPLACEMENT, REVISITED

Augmentation was discussed earlier in the AI adoption mindset chapter (Chapter 10). Because of the points made earlier, the best way to think about expectations with AI is that machines work best when they augment the work of humans. There are certainly cases where a machine or software can replace some or even most of a human's job, but it could be argued then that that job was never a good fit for a human in the first place. After all, humans are not great at highly repetitive tasks with little room for creativity, insights, and improvement.

AI, then, is here to help, not replace. In marketing work, it's advisable to find the areas where the team struggles because the work is drudgery or there is a high rate of errors, and, instead, find ways to automate those and focus team members on creative problem-solving and the task of tying concepts and ideas together.

BIAS AND AI

For a thorough exploration of the issues of bias and artificial intelligence, it is recommended that one read books and articles solely dedicated to this topic, which may provide a level of depth that this book does not. But it is important to cover this at least at a high level here. AI and, more specifically, machine learning goes through a process of doing just that—learning—based on the inputs given to it.

Thus, if the platform is taught to recognize humans versus inanimate objects by only showing pictures of Caucasian males, it should come as no surprise if it starts making mistakes when asked to detect humans with different skin tones, genders, or other, perhaps even subtle differences. For instance, a paper by researchers from MIT and Stanford [HARDESTY18] found that AI programs' error rates in determining the gender of light-skinned men never reached 1%, but for darker-skinned women, they were as high as 34%.[3]

Or in a purely text-based application, Amazon built a resumé reviewing tool to screen applicants' resumés that launched in 2014, which ended up discriminating against nonmale candidates and was ultimately scrapped because of the bias it introduced into the hiring process [DASTIN18].[4]

Additionally, tools like ChatGPT are primarily trained on text written in English, creating a bias toward content written in a single language. This includes biased information appearing as text, of course, but also in images and video applications. For instance, Google partnered with Harvard University sociologist Ellis Monk to create a ten-tone palette of skin tones used by its Google Meets video chat application to better serve people of color [REU22].[5] Other video chat companies have been under fire for similar issues, which stem from the inputs. The term GIGO or "garbage in, garbage out" is used in the software world and can be applied here as well. If one inputs a very select or biased set of data, AI will assume that it is the universe of possible data, thus creating a biased start. It should be no surprise, then, that "garbage out" is what occurs with biased results.

What to Watch Out For

AI tools are being made available to everyone, but incorrectly applied tools can be problematic or worse. Thus, there are a few things to watch out for as you plan greater AI adoption within your marketing organization or elsewhere.

When discussing tools like machine learning, the name itself implies that there is a starting point from which the technology grows and ultimately *learns* along the way. What is fed into that machine learning process makes a huge difference in the delivered outcomes.

Although there are others within an organization that may have a part in the integrity of data, marketers should be aware of potentially problematic areas, and ensuring that source data is fair and unbiased is a good place to start. Marketers should work with their data and IT teams to make sure that, where possible, data sources include the full spectrum of information, and that any potential biases are discussed and documented, in the interest of transparency. Furthermore, all parties need to acknowledge that the introduction of bias into systems isn't a one-time occurrence, but can often be part of a long-term, often unintentional yet systematic set of processes that allow small changes to go undetected. Thus, organizations, need to remain vigilant with potential sources of bias, and the proliferation of bias within systems.

This short section of the book does not do the topic of bias in AI justice, but suffice it to say it is a very important topic and one that readers need to keep in mind as they proceed with any initiatives and investments. This also leads to the next point.

Transparency

The latest artificial intelligence-based platform or tool gives some really interesting and compelling insights and results, but how exactly is it arriving at those endpoints? This is where transparency comes into play.

Artificial intelligence and machine learning often provide results with little to no insight into how they reach their conclusions or recommendations. This leads to the "black box" problem that marketers and others at organizations often find themselves faced with. They like the results and want to trust them, but the algorithms that reach these conclusions are obfuscated and opaque.

Thus, users should strive to find AI tools that offer transparency in their decision-making. Many simple algorithm and workflow automation tools are simple enough to understand and even to program for noncoders. But when the outcomes are critical and can alienate or disenfranchise parts of the audience or the population, this lack of transparency and the bias that can be embedded within decisions can be dangerous.

For instance, how are predictions and offers being given to people based on their race or ethnicity, gender, sexual orientation, or other factors that can be discriminatory? Could the discrimination be subtler than a label or category that is easy to detect, such as their surname or zip code within a city?

All of these need to be considered when relying more heavily on AI to automate large parts of marketing.

WHAT TO DO ABOUT BIAS AND AI?

Transparency is key and must be a foundational component of any AI initiative. It's important to know what data is being used, how it's being interpreted, and whether the results are reliable. As much as possible, try to ensure that datasets equitably represent all parts of society. Additionally, tools like fairness metrics can help provide feedback.

Additionally, it can be beneficial to have an audit process in place, depending on the situation. This ensures that the AI system is operating as intended and doesn't contain any unintended biases or inaccuracies. Additionally, having a third-party look at the AI system's results and code can provide valuable feedback that may have otherwise gone unnoticed.

This requires deeper discussions and working in tandem with data science teams and other partners within an organization to better understand and mitigate against bias as soon as it's detected.

IT'S TIME TO RESKILL AND UPSKILL

Although the idea that humans will all be out of work due to robots within a few years is simply overblown and unrealistic, that doesn't mean people don't need to rethink their relationships to work. Thus, it's time to adjust skills to be most relevant in a world driven by artificial intelligence.

This doesn't actually mean that everyone needs to become a data scientist or software engineer. Much to the contrary, those are some areas where AI will continue to take over parts of roles in the coming years. Instead, it is time to rethink roles and skillsets in terms of how AI tools can help do tasks better, quicker, and more efficiently. With the plethora of tools available, people should be able to try this out fairly quickly, easily, and inexpensively at first, so they can determine which types of tools and platforms can be most effective for them and their marketing team.

CONCLUSION

Readers chose this book because they see the power and potential of artificial intelligence to improve marketing and make it more effective, and that is most certainly the case. To be even more successful, it is also critical to keep in mind some of the mindsets and potential pitfalls relying on artificial intelligence can bring. By being mindful of bias and transparency and the ideal way that AI and human intelligence can work together, marketing teams will be set up for the greatest chance of success.

NOTES

1   [DIG23] Dig Insights. "Automation Was Estimated to Replace 30% of Jobs by 2030, and That Was Before COVID-19 Hit." Dig Insights. Retrieved March 4, 2023 from https://diginsights.com/resources/blog/automation-was-estimated-to-replace-30-of-jobs-by-2030-and-that-was-before-covid-19-hit/.

2   [CIO23] CIO Look. "Robots or Humans, Who Will Take Over the Jobs?" CIO Look blog. Retrieved March 4, 2023 from https://ciolook.com/robots-or-humans-who-will-take-over-the-jobs/#:~:text=The%20World%20Economic%20Forum%20reported,employment%20being%20generated%20by%202025.

3   [HARDESTY18] Hardesty, Larry. "Study Finds Gender and Skin-Type Bias in Commercial Artificial Intelligence Systems." MIT News. February 11, 2018. Retrieved March 4, from https://news.mit.edu/2018/study-finds-gender-skin-type-bias-artificial-intelligence-systems-0212.

4   [DASTIN18] Dastin, Jeffrey. "Amazon Scraps Secret AI Recruiting Tool That Showed Bias Against Women." Reuters. October 10, 2018. Retrieved March 4, 2023 from https://www.reuters.com/article/us-amazon-com-jobs-automation-insight/amazon-scraps-secret-ai-recruiting-tool-that-showed-bias-against-women-idUSKCN1MK08G.

5   [REU22] Reuters. "Google Unveils a New 10-Shade Skin Tone Scale to Try to Remove Racial Bias from Its AI Tools." Reuters. Retrieved March 4, 2023 from https://www.euronews.com/next/2022/05/12/google-unveils-a-new-10-shade-skin-tone-scale-to-try-to-remove-racial-bias-from-its-ai-too.

EPILOGUE

A lot of ground has been covered in this book! AI can help marketers in many ways, from strategy to implementation to analysis and insights. Despite all this promise, it takes a careful and thoughtful approach to ensure it is implemented meaningfully, improving the understanding a brand has of its customers, the experience those customers have, and the business results. One thing is for certain: this is a fast-changing field, and we're not even close to seeing the last of the innovations in this space, as the amount of venture capital (VC) money and media hype around AI would suggest.

But hype and VC money alone aren't good reasons for marketers to pay attention, particularly the amount of attention that AI seems to be taking in the general zeitgeist. Following are the key potential benefits that AI can bring to marketers:

- Saving time, effort, and redundant work so marketers can focus on more strategic work

- Improving marketers' understanding of customers to drive more relevant offers and experiences

- Improving the customer experience through personalized content, customer journeys, and next-best-action approaches

- Enabling better audience segmentation and insights so that marketers can continuously improve their work

Now, the work begins, or more likely, continues, since it's unlikely that you're not using at least a few of the methods of AI-enabled marketing discussed so far. This guide wraps up by talking a little about some ways that strategic marketing leaders and teams should think about artificial intelligence in the months ahead.

For those who are reading this book to consider how to harness the power of AI in their marketing and customer experience, here are four recommended starting points:

1. Establish guidelines and company-specific best practices on when, how, and why generative AI tools can and can *not* be used in the work performed by your teams. Tools like ChatGPT, DALL-E, and others can be incredibly beneficial when applied to solve the right challenges.

2. Embrace an AI-driven digital experience analytics platform that empowers businesses to proactively identify and resolve issues derived from customer feedback and interaction data. This enables you to stay ahead of problems and ensure a seamless customer journey.

3. Prioritize a self-service model that caters to customer expectations of instant issue resolution. By implementing chatbots, dynamic FAQs, and semantic search engines, you can empower customers to find answers effortlessly, without relying heavily on customer service representatives.

4. Unlock the power of personalized experiences for each customer. Research shows that nearly three-quarters of customers expect tailored interactions. Failing to deliver on those expectations can lead to customer frustration and dissatisfaction.

By following these recommendations, it's possible to elevate marketing and customer experience strategies to new heights, ensuring long-term success and customer satisfaction.

As a last thought, readers should focus again more on the mindset shifts rather than the technologies themselves. Although the author endeavored to get this book ready for launch as expeditiously as possible, even in the weeks between finishing the final edits and this book being available to readers today, there have been many changes, updates, and other happenings in this space.

What *hasn't* changed and is unlikely to change are the ways that marketers should think about embracing AI and related technologies and approaches. To reiterate, here are those four aspects again:

1. **Augmentation, not replacement.** AI and its many forms—from algorithms to natural language processing, machine learning, and more—is best thought of as a powerful assistive technology to humans and not as something that will take the place of the most "human" parts of our jobs. That means strategy, creativity, innovation, and tying together lots of big ideas are still in the realm of the human workforce and will be for quite a while.

2. **Starting, not finishing.** Don't send a request to AI to write, create, analyze, or do another critical task and expect it to be perfect and ready for prime time. Granted, it can get users 25%, 50%, or even 75% of the way there, but a human will still be needed to get it across the finish line or, at the very least, double-check that it is ready to go. Remember that bias is still rampant in certain areas of AI, and the lack of transparency in many machine learning models makes it difficult to predict the outcomes when AI is simply set loose.

3. **Curation, not summarization.** AI can do a great job pulling many references, sources, and pieces of information from across the Web, an internal archive, or other sources. Yet, it may not do a great job at creating the type of summary of all of that curated information if there are very specific needs. For instance, a marketing team needs to look at information in a very specific way, which a general-purpose AI will fail to live up to. Thus, a curator is a good role for an AI, while creating a strategic summary of the information that considers the nuances of a brand, industry, and customer base is something that a human will need to contribute to significantly.

4. **Analysis, not strategy.** Want large amounts of structured and unstructured data crawled and analyzed? Great, AI is well-suited for this task. Just don't expect artificial intelligence to then come up with a unique or well-suited strategy for your marketing efforts.

Strategy and creativity, in general, are still realms where humans reign supreme, and AI is again an augmentation of some of the areas where humans are lacking.

In the months ahead, there will surely be countless new opportunities and challenges. Hopefully readers found some ideas, insights, and thoughts to share with their teams to help implement the most meaningful types of AI for their business, team, and customers. It's time to move forward together!

INDEX

www.ingramcontent.com/pod-product-compliance
Lightning Source LLC
La Vergne TN
LVHW022320060326
832902LV00020B/3584